CW01660056

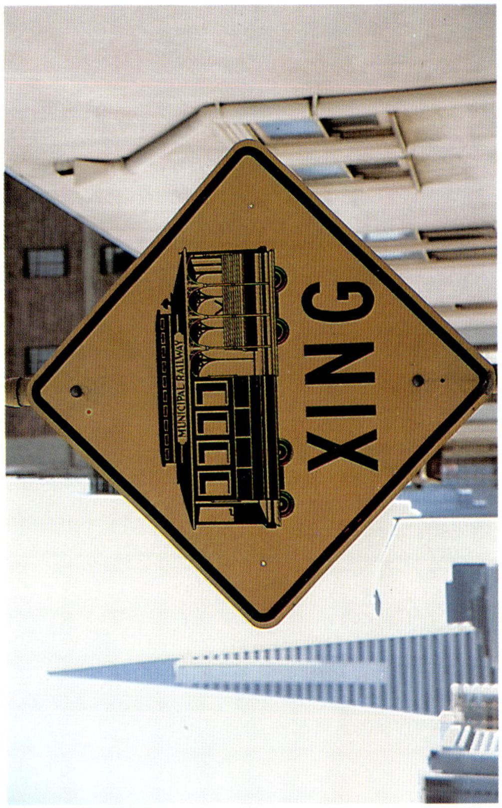
MUNICIPAL RAILWAY
XING

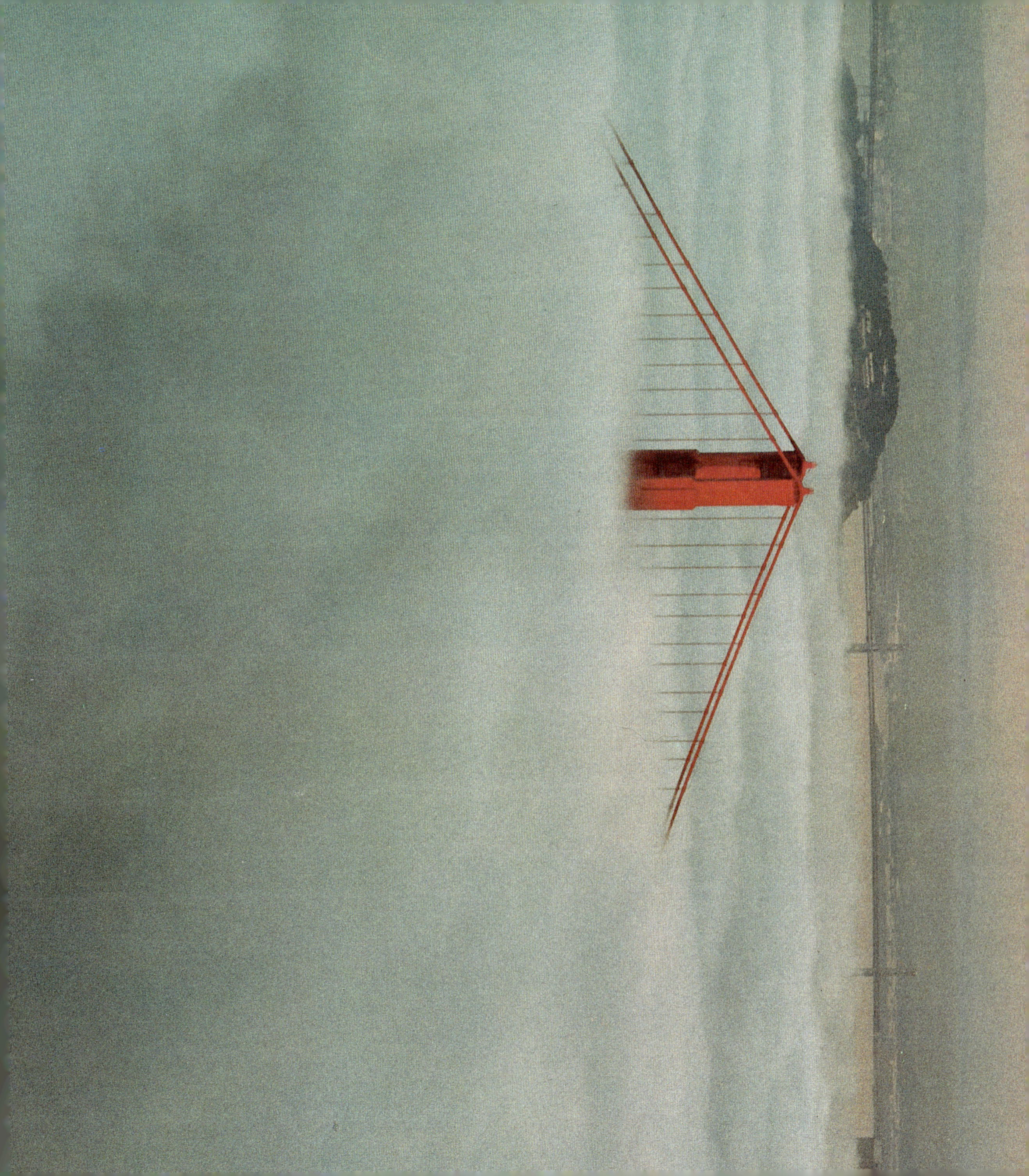

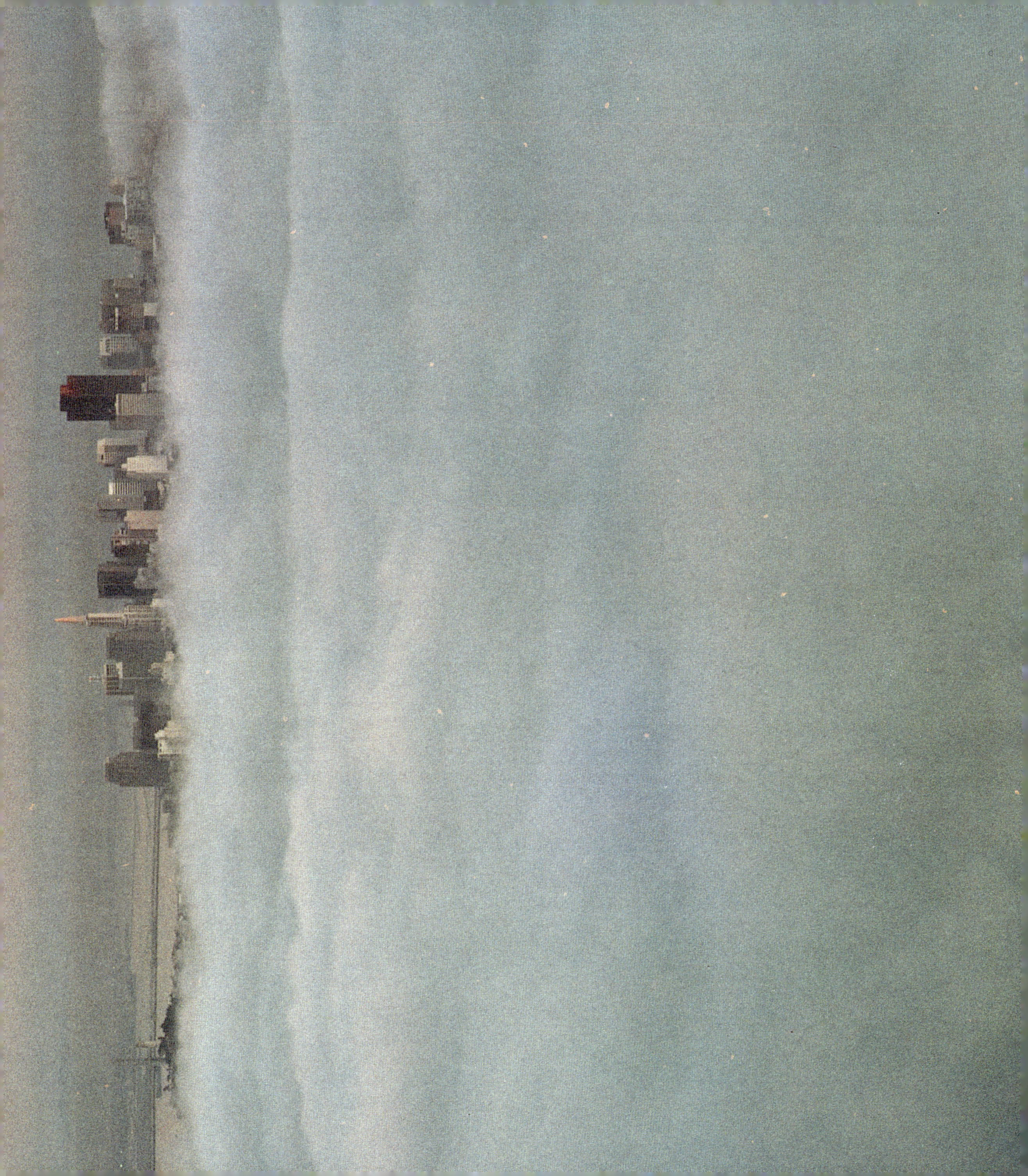

Illustrations credits:
Archivio White Star/Marcello Bertinetti:
Cover, pages 7, 8-9, 15, 16-17, 21, 23, 29, 30-31, 32, 36, 38, 38, 39 top, 42, 45, 46-47, 48, 50-51, 52, 55, 61, 63, 65, 68, 73, 74, 76-77, 78, 83, 84-85, 88, 90, 91, 93, 94-95.
Archivio White Star/Carlo De Fabianis:
Pages 6, 13, 14, 19, 22, 28, 34, 37, 43 bottom, 54, 58, 60, 62, 71, 75, 86, 87.
Archivio White Star/Angela White Bertinetti:
Back cover, pages 1, 12, 18, 20, 25, 33, 35, 39 bottom, 43 top, 44, 53, 56, 57, 59, 64, 70, 72, 79, 82, 89, 92, 96.
Dallas & John Eaton/Apa Photo Agency:
Pages 11, 40, 81.
Kotott/Zefa:
Page 49.
Ben Nakayama/Apa Photo Agency:
Page 26.
Michel Reanaudeau/Hoa-Qui:
Page 4.
David Ryan/Apa Photo Agency:
Pages 66, 67.
Piergiorgio Sclarandis/Focus Team:
Pages 10, 27.
Adina Tony/Apa Photo Agency:
Pages 41, 80.
Yvan Travert/Hoa-Qui:
Page 24.

© White Star
Via C. Sassone 24, Vercelli, Italy.

All rights reserved. Reproduction of the whole or any part of the contents, without written permission, is prohibited.

Printed and bound in Singapore.

First published in English in 1991 by
Tiger Books International PLC, London.
ISBN 1-85501-173-5

Translated by
Patricia Borlenghi

Edited by
Heather Thomas

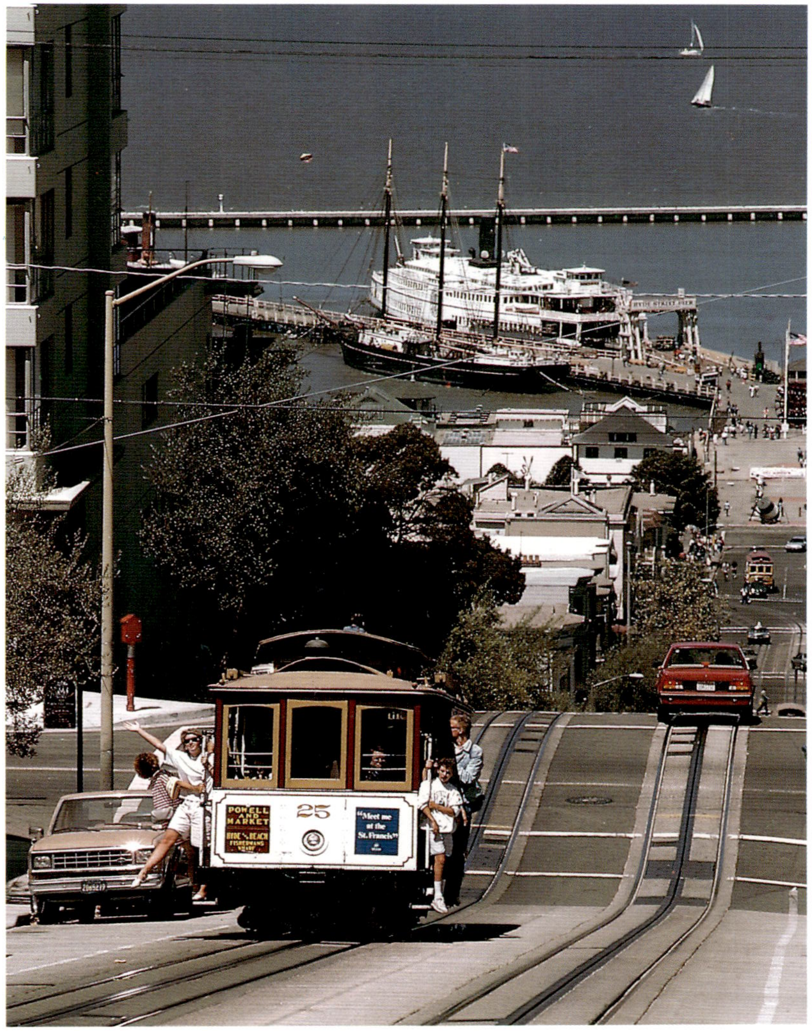

INSIDE SAN FRANCISCO

TEXT
FABIO BOURBON

DESIGN
PATRIZIA BALOCCO

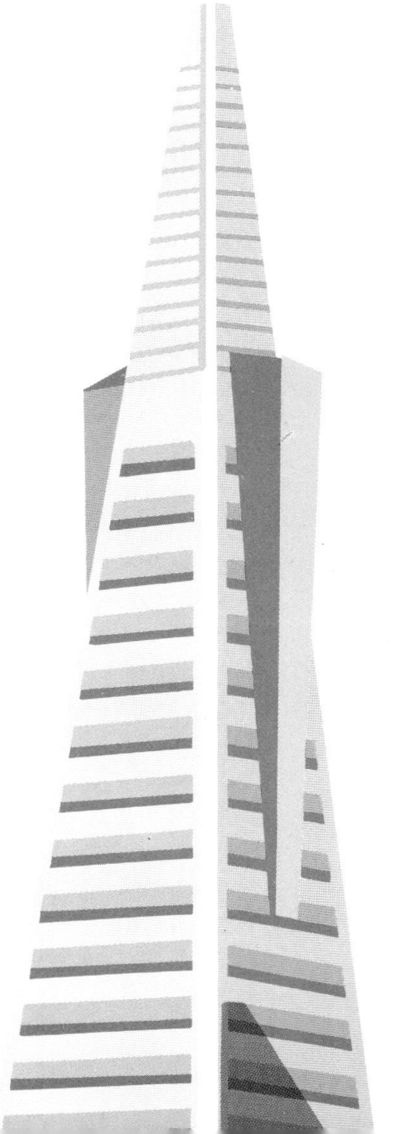

TIGER BOOKS INTERNATIONAL

2-3 A distinctive red tower of the world-famous Golden Gate Bridge rises from the morning fog that often envelops the Bay Area in the summer months. However, this damp ocean mist usually melts away by mid-morning when the blue skies and the sunshine return.

4 San Francisco is famous for its clanging cable cars which have been immortalized in song. In 1964, the cable cars were declared a National Historic Landmark, and three lines still operate out of the original network which in 1900 covered over 100 miles of track.

6 In the blue waters of the Bay is the infamous island of Alcatraz which was once a notorious federal prison. You can still tour the cell blocks and guard towers of this chilling place which once housed Al Capone and the Birdman of Alcatraz.

7 Telegraph Hill is dominated by the Coit Tower – a monument to the city's firefighters. Inside this unusual building, you can view an astonishing array of frescos and murals illustrating scenes from Californian labor in the 1930s which were painted by twenty-five artists in 1934 under the inspiration of Diego Rivera.

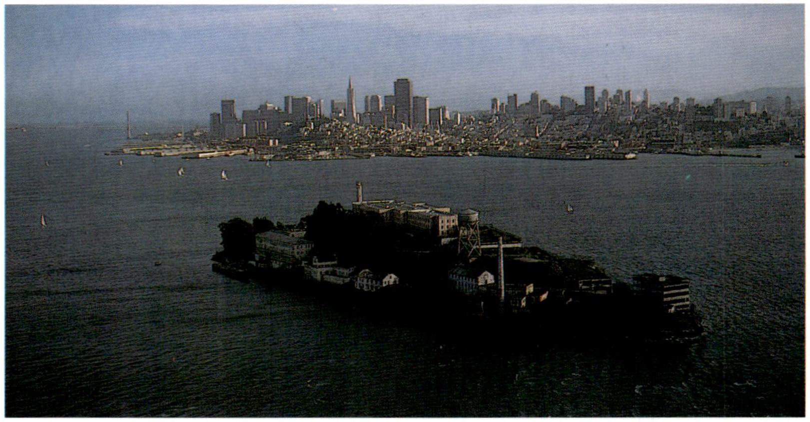

San Francisco's story starts over 200 years ago in 1776 when Spanish missionaries established the Mission San Francisco de Asis there. Spanish, English and Russian traders settled in the Bay area over the next few decades but it was not until 1848 with the discovery of gold that San Francisco's population rocketed – from 800 to 25,000 within just two years. The 'Forty-Niners' poured into the muddy shanty town, fired by the prospect of finding gold and getting rich, and it was soon transformed into a bustling city. There is a story that during the Gold Rush many miners sent their laundry to China to be washed because it was more economic to send it to the other side of the Pacific than to get it laundered in the city where prices for the most trivial everyday services were exorbitant! In those same pioneering days, a barber could make a fortune by cutting the hair of gold miners and sifting through their felled locks for precious gold dust! San Francisco has always been a very special city, owing its charm to a combination of different factors: its magnificent location, its temperate climate and, above all, its people who have a unique and inimitable lifestyle. Imagination, flair, non-conformity, radicalism and hospitality are the hallmarks of this most cosmopolitan of cities, where even the police cars proudly display a sign: 'At your service'. The residents are justly proud of their beautiful city and are always ready to talk about it enthusiastically at every opportunity. The locals whom you will encounter in any bar or café will lose no time in engaging you in friendly conversation and are extremely hospitable and helpful to visitors. The city is built on twenty-one hills and boasts the steepest streets in the world. It is the most multi-racial of all America's cities and possesses more restaurants than any other urban conurbation in the United States with the sole exception of New York. Yet, surprisingly, San Francisco is a relatively small city built on a peninsula with the blue waters of the Bay and the sea on three sides. Extending over the tip of this peninsula overlooking the Bay is the uniform grid system of downtown streets which is dominated by the instantly recognisable Transamerica Pyramid, which with fifty-two floors is the tallest skyscraper in the city, and by the fluted Coit Tower high on Telegraph Hill, which was built in 1934 as a bequest from Mrs Lillie Hitchcock Coit, an eccentric millionairess and volunteer firefighter, to honour the city's heroic firemen. She was just one of the eccentric characters who, with their generosity and inventiveness, truly embodied the spirit of San Francisco. In fact, originality is a predominant feature of Californian style and architecture. You have only to explore the steep hills of the city decorated with brightly painted and bizarre Victorian residences to see this for yourself. Unique in their genre and fondly referred to by the locals as the 'Painted Ladies', these multi-colored houses reflect the city's individualistic and extravagant character and emphasise its residents' proud attachment to the traditions of the past.

The numerous well-tended flower beds and floral displays in the city's parks and on street corners are eloquent testimony to the San Franciscans' passion for greenery and gardening. It is not unusual to see people after a busy day at the office, weeding and planting out the flower beds and borders and tending the little lawns in front of their vividly decorated houses with meticulous and loving care.

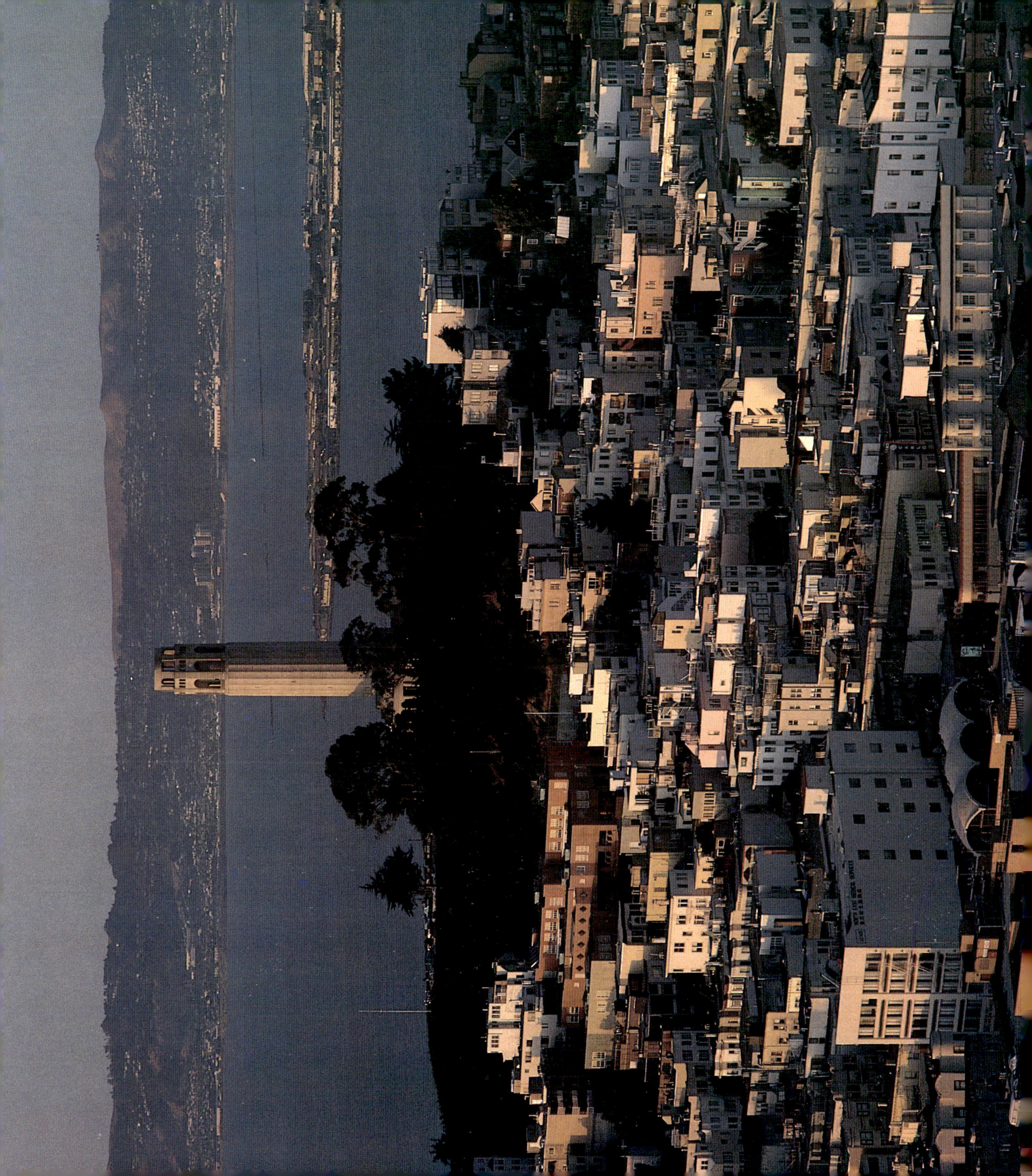

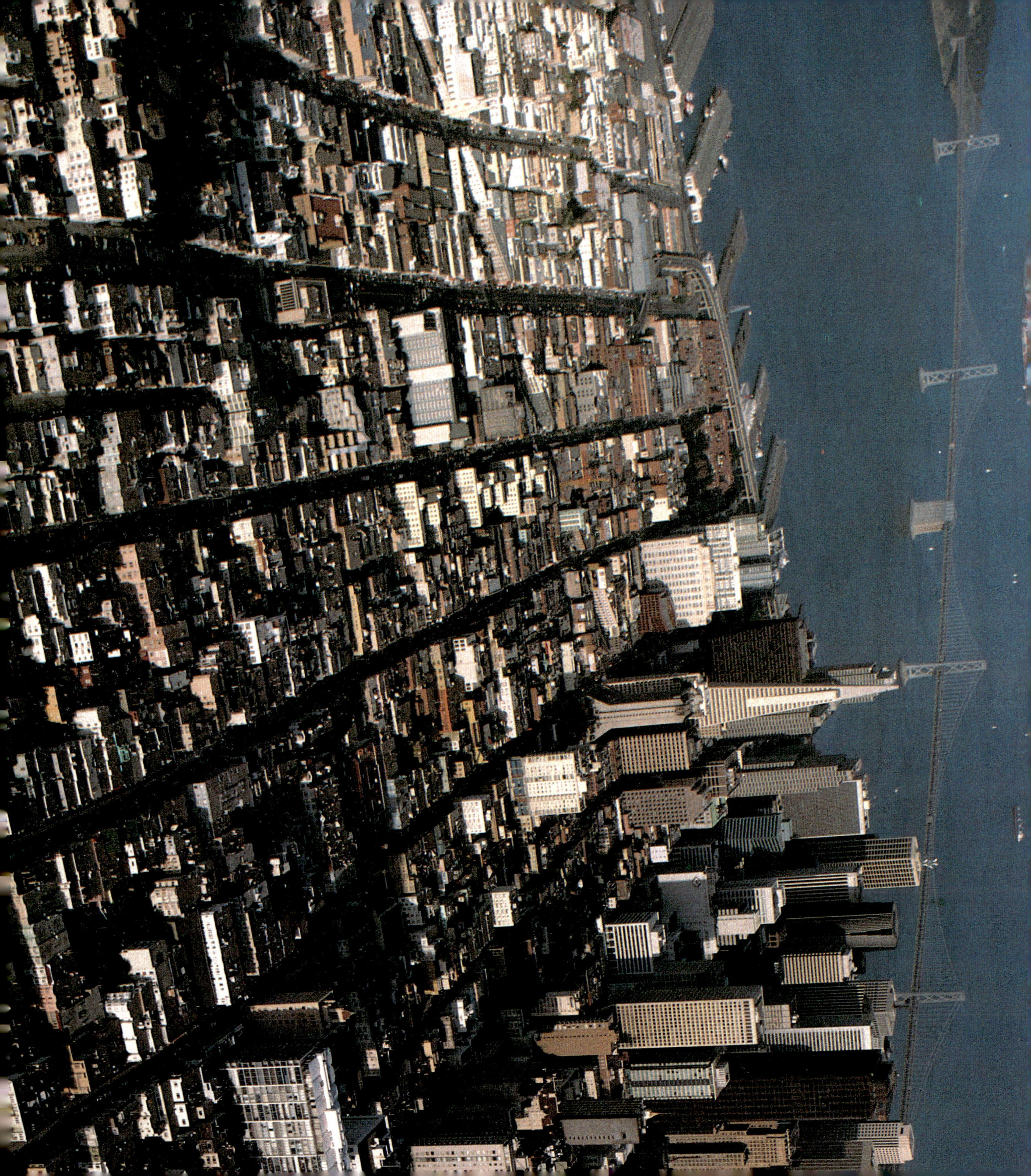

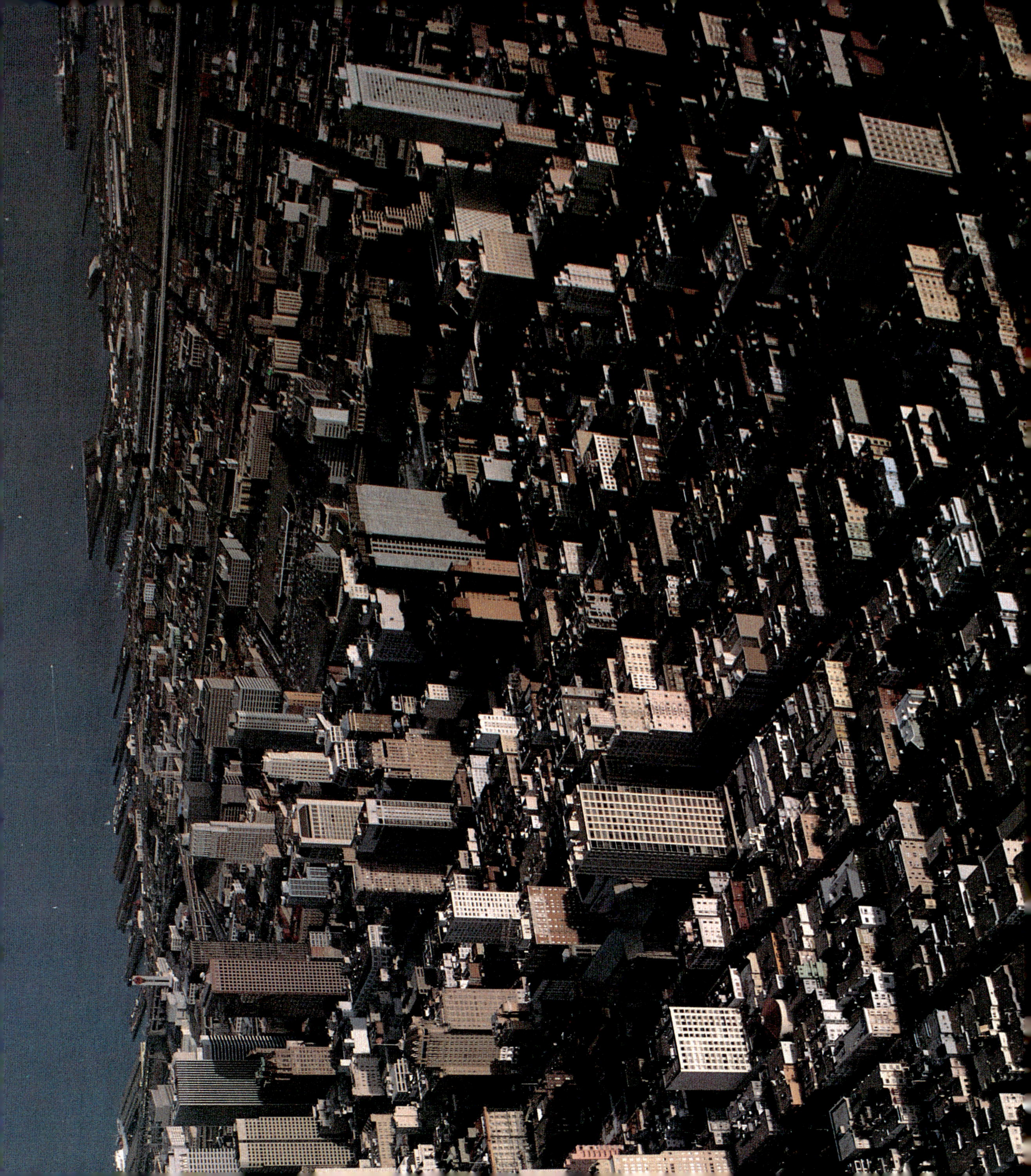

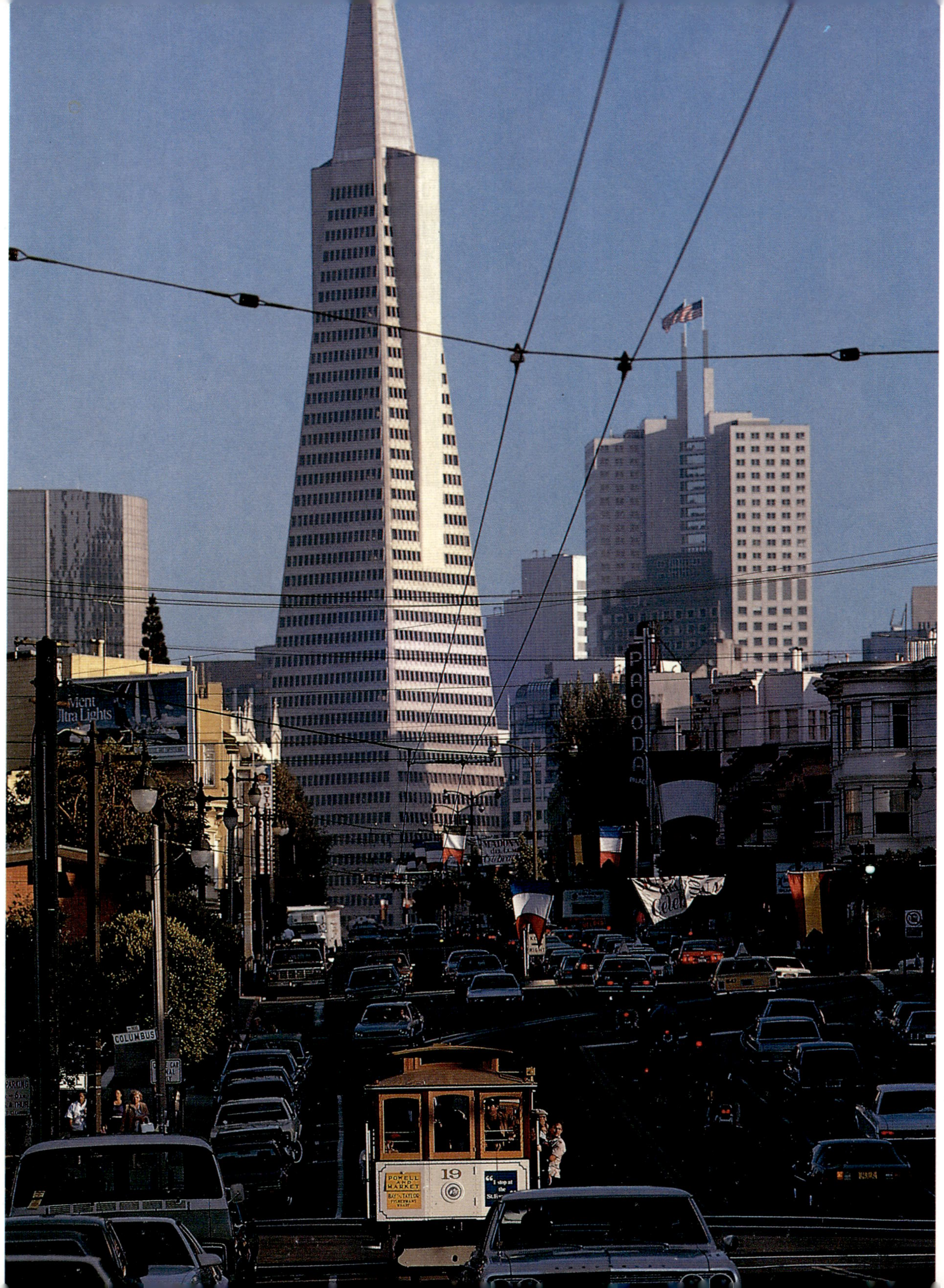

8-9 In spite of its history of earthquakes, the downtown area and Financial District of the city are dominated by tall skyscrapers which have been designed and constructed using the most advanced anti-earthquake technology available. Note particularly the Transamerica Pyramid on the left – the tallest building in San Francisco.

10 When the Transamerica Pyramid was completed in 1972, many San Franciscans were upset by its unorthodox appearance and criticised it for not blending in with or complementing the existing architectural styles in the city. In fact, it was nicknamed unkindly 'the great alien ring toss'. Today, however, this original building has become a much loved symbol of the city and a distinctive feature of the San Francisco skyline.

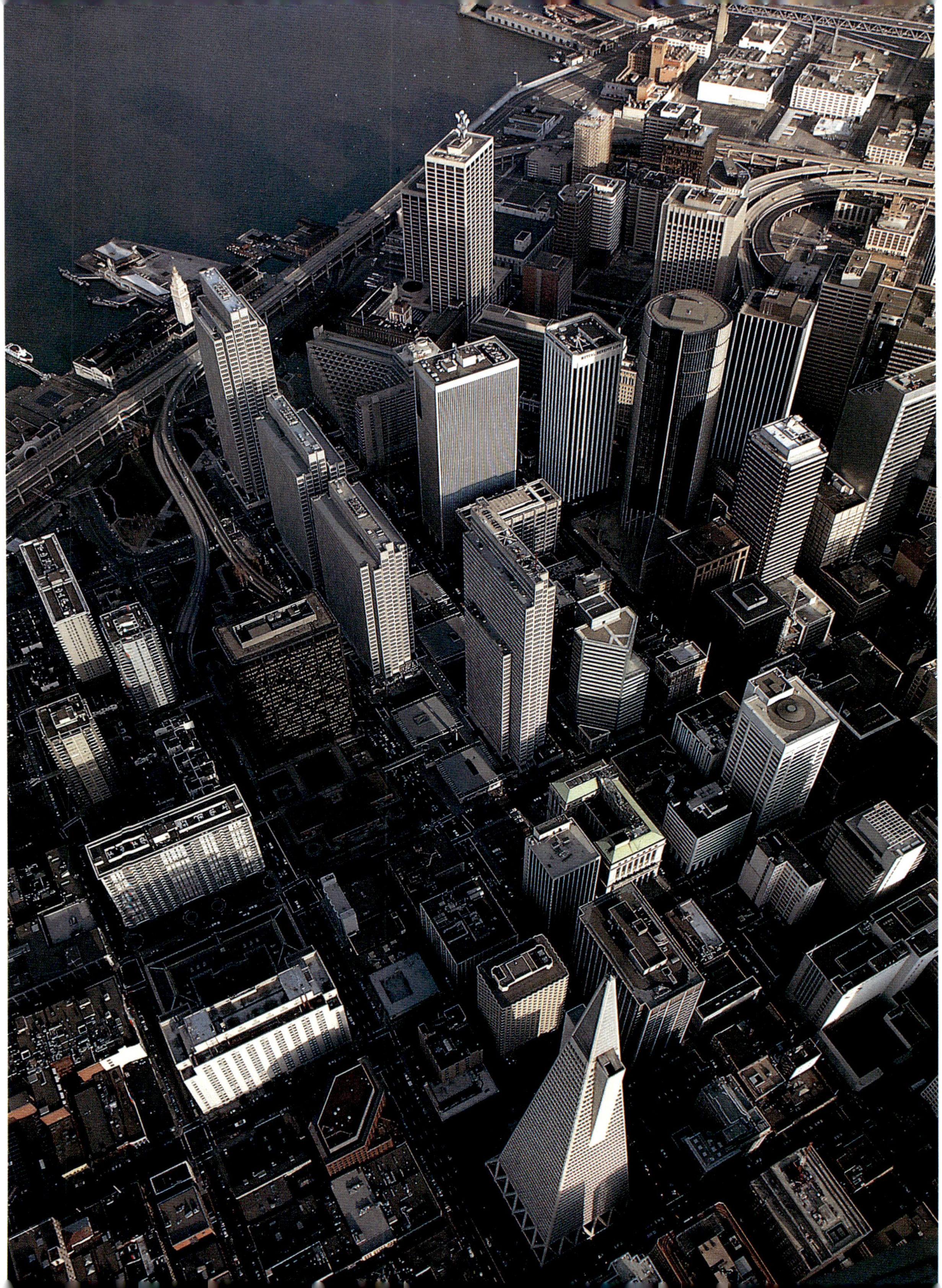

15 This aerial view of the Financial District is evidence of the enormous increase in skyscrapers in recent years, so much so that San Francisco has become the 'Manhattan' of the West Coast.

16-17 Lombard Street with its hairpin bends and brightly colored flowerbeds is the most winding and spectacular of all San Francisco's streets, and perhaps the most crooked in the world. Pedestrians can ascend the 40-degree slope by way of some steps.

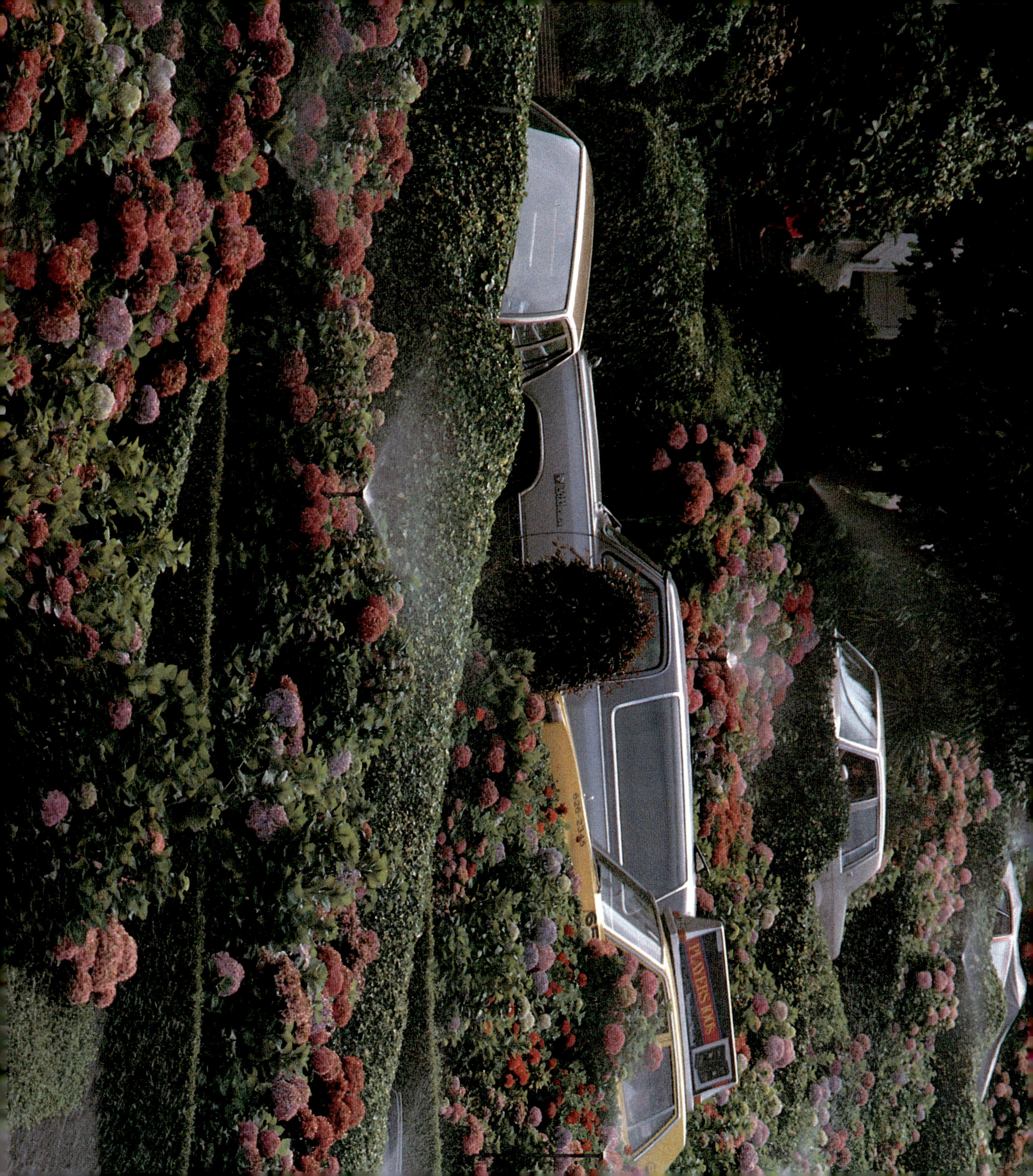

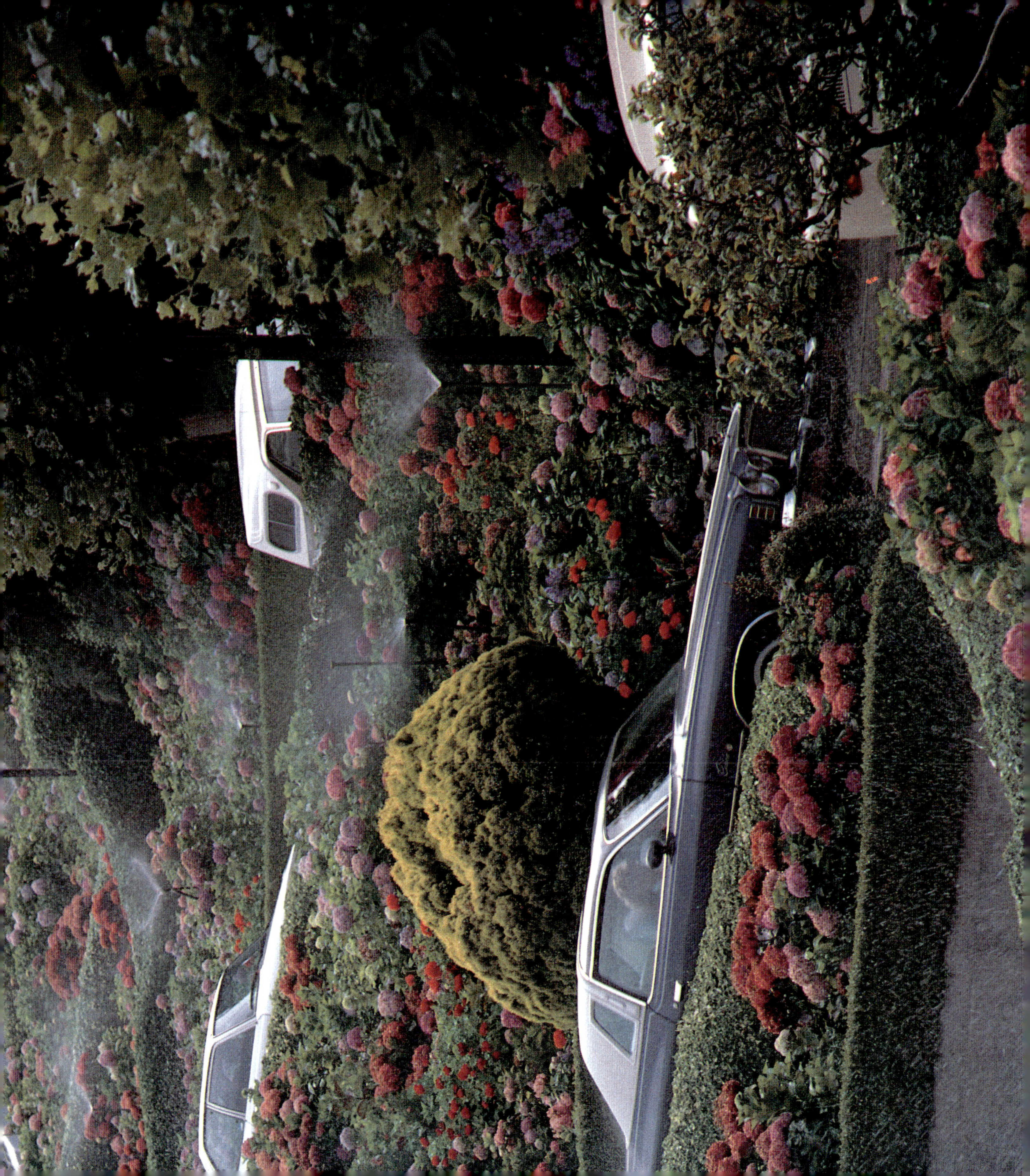

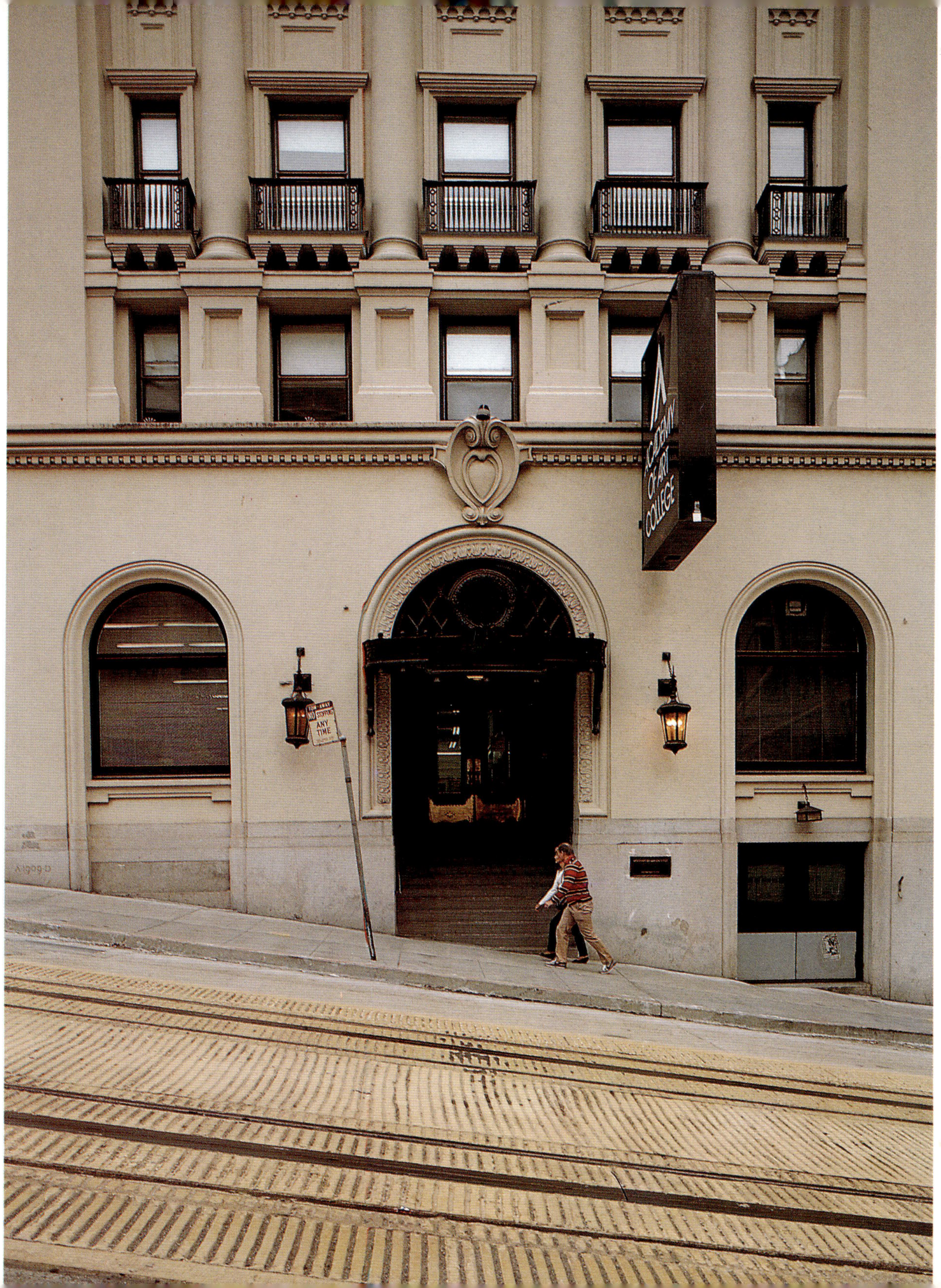

18 Because of the remarkable steepness of many of the streets, it is not unusual for many buildings to be asymmetrical and taller on one side than on the other. Hills are an inescapable challenge to visitors and residents alike, and a good comfortable pair of walking shoes is essential if you plan to explore the city on foot.

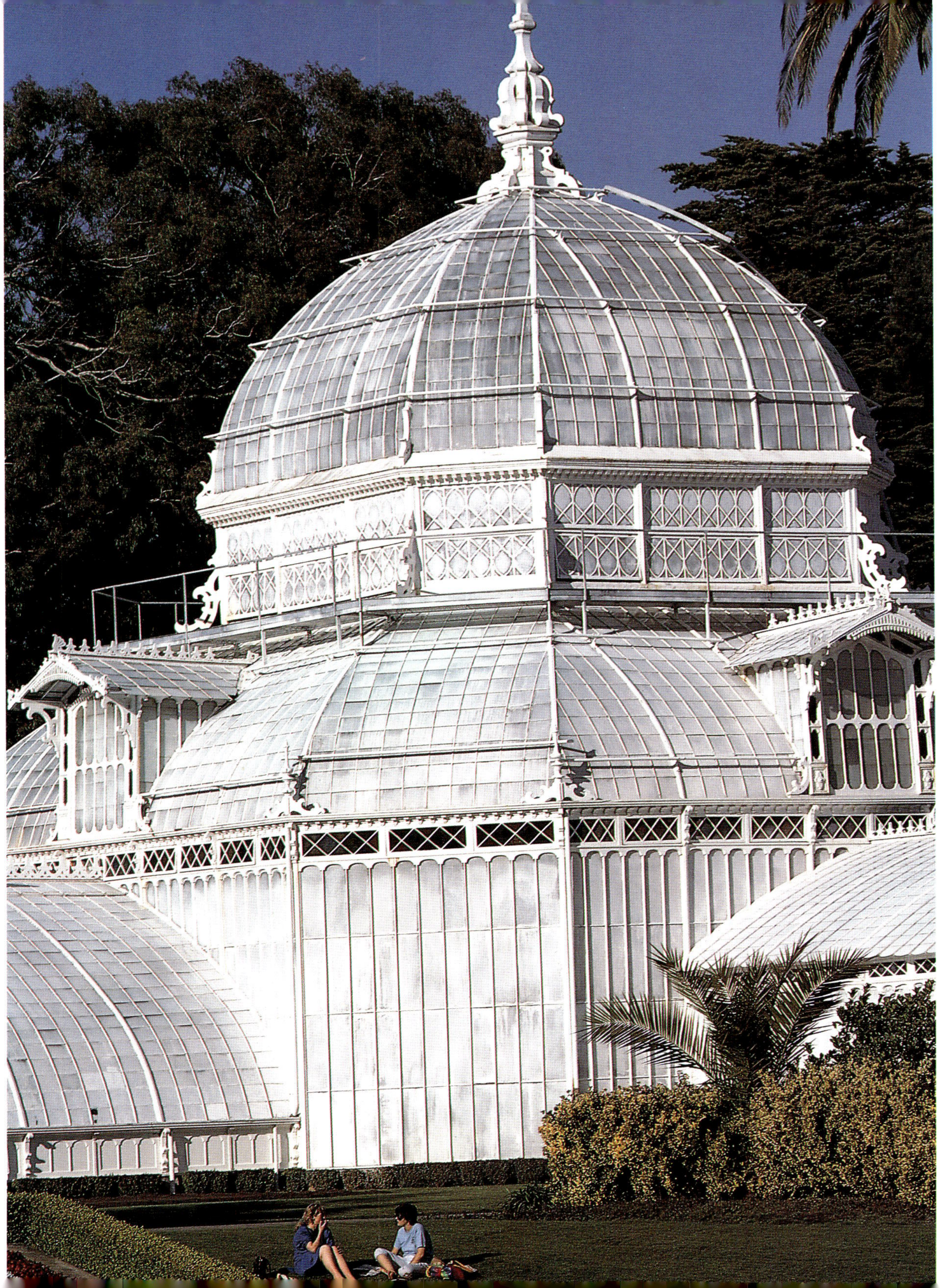

28 The port of San Francisco has gradually lost much of its past commercial importance, and today fewer merchant and cargo ships dock there.

29 Telegraph Hill rises to about 300 feet and is crowned by the Coit Tower whose silhouette can be seen here. This is one of the most elegant residential districts of San Francisco.

30-31 Since its inauguration in 1937, the Golden Gate Bridge has become the most enduring symbol of San Francisco. In constructing the bridge, its designer, Joseph Strauss, had to overcome formidable obstacles including high winds, fast currents, shallow channels, shortage of funding and the so-called earthquake mentality of the bridge's many opponents.

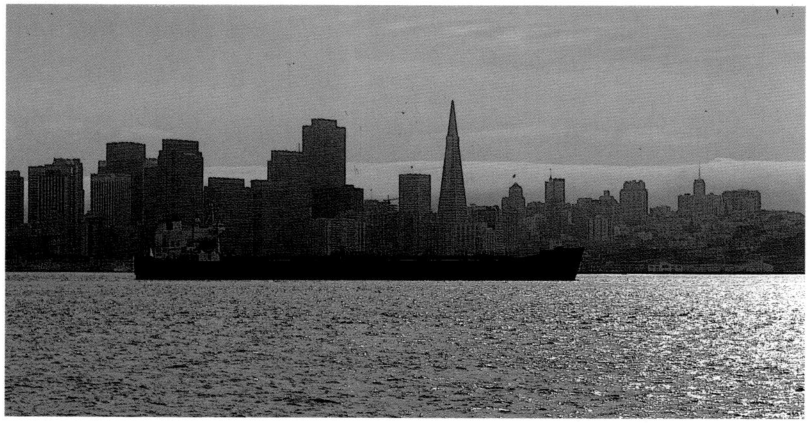

At the foot of the south tower of the Golden Gate Bridge is Fort Point, built between 1853 and 1861 by US Army engineers to protect San Francisco and access to the Bay during the Civil War. When designing the bridge, Strauss deliberately created an arch within the structure to conserve the fort; today it is a military museum, and National Park Rangers in Civil War uniforms offer guided tours and cannon demonstrations. Fort Point is perfectly preserved, probably because it was never attacked, unlike the nearby Presidio, a huge military post now transformed into a 1500-acre park of fields and woods. The Spanish built the garrison in 1776, but the only original building that remains is the Commandante's headquarters which is now an Officers' Club, and the oldest building in San Francisco. The red-brick barracks, surrounded by trees, represents part of the living history of San Francisco, while the Presidio Army Museum houses the records of the battles and the struggles fought during the Spanish occupation. The Presidio is still the headquarters of the US Sixth Army.

On the waterfront down in the port, east of Fisherman's Wharf, is the Ferry Building from which a great fleet of ferries once set out to link the city with the islands in the bay and the far-flung suburbs. Nearby is the grandiose Embarcadero Center with its four high-rise towers which offer the visitor a wide choice of shops, boutiques and high-class restaurants. In nearby Montgomery and California Streets there are skyscrapers of dizzy heights. This is where the largest banks, insurance companies, big corporations and financial institutions on the West Coast are located. Not far from Union Square is Japantown where you can find shops selling Japanese electrical goods, pearls and kimonos, as well as the most renowned and popular Japanese restaurants. You can sample authentic Japanese cooking or relax in one of the popular sushi bars over a glass of sake, produced not in Japan but in Berkeley! If the pleasures of shopping prove too tiring, then there is no better way of unwinding than to visit one of the traditional communal baths which specialize in shiatsu, a massage technique which focuses on the pressure points of the body to ease tension and refresh the spirit.

Another San Francisco curiosity is Pier 39, an old waterfront area that has been developed to create a shopping mall of boutiques specializing in crystal glass, leathergoods, Americana, tapestries, quilts and decorations for the home. Dozens of buskers entertain passers-by with improvised and often entertaining acts. The many quayside restaurants provide an infinite variety of choice, each offering a spectacular view of the Bay dotted with a myriad of white sails. The local speciality is sole accompanied by an exquisite Californian chardonnay from the nearby vineyards of the Napa and Sonoma Valleys, followed by strawberries in chocolate sauce for dessert. Along Jefferson Street is the most popular as well as the oldest stretch of the seafront which is always thronged with visitors who crowd into the souvenir shops, the seafood restaurants, the Maritime Museum and along the old piers from which the frequent boat trips depart every day on sightseeing tours of the Bay and the island of Alcatraz, once a federal penitentiary.

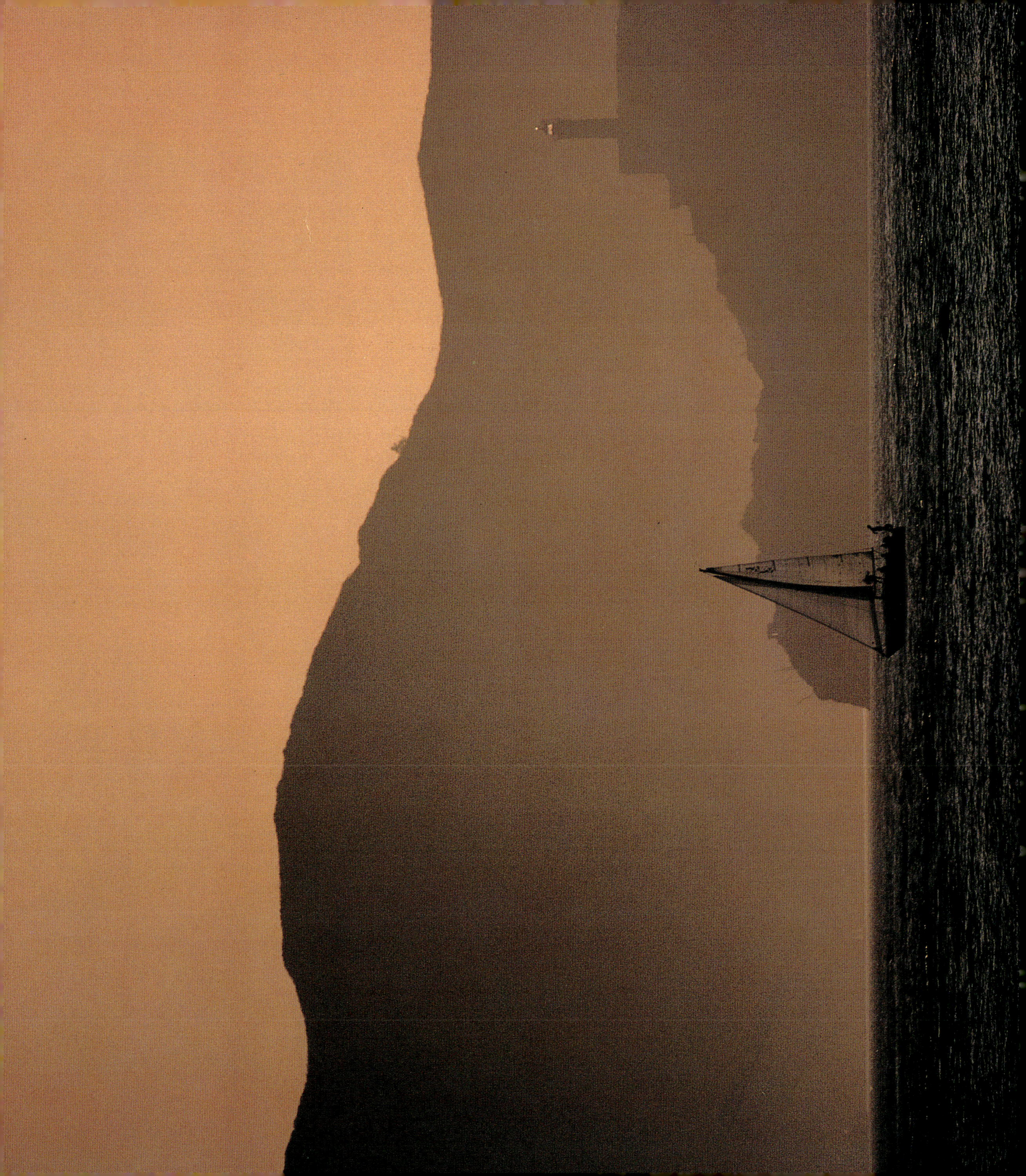

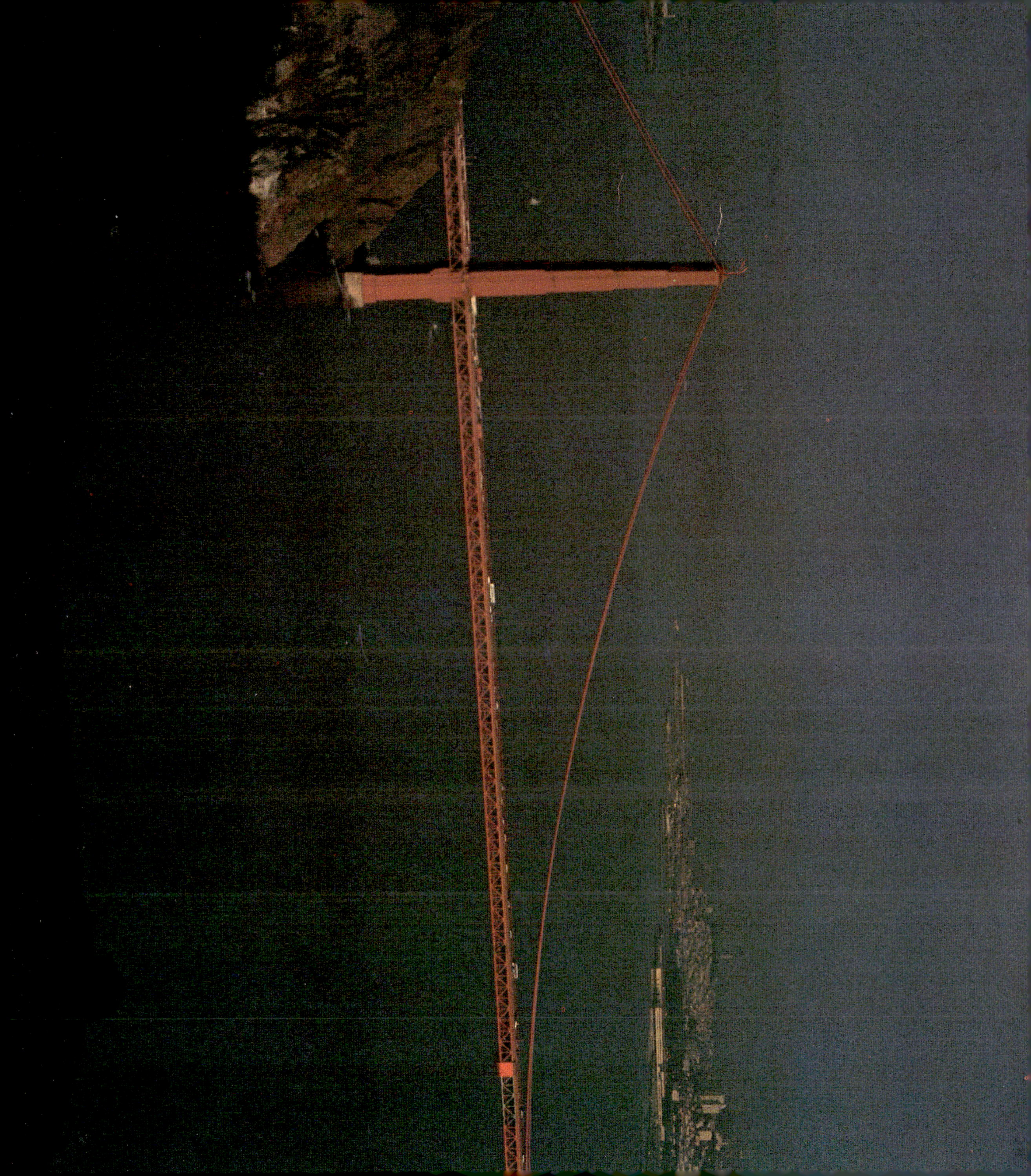

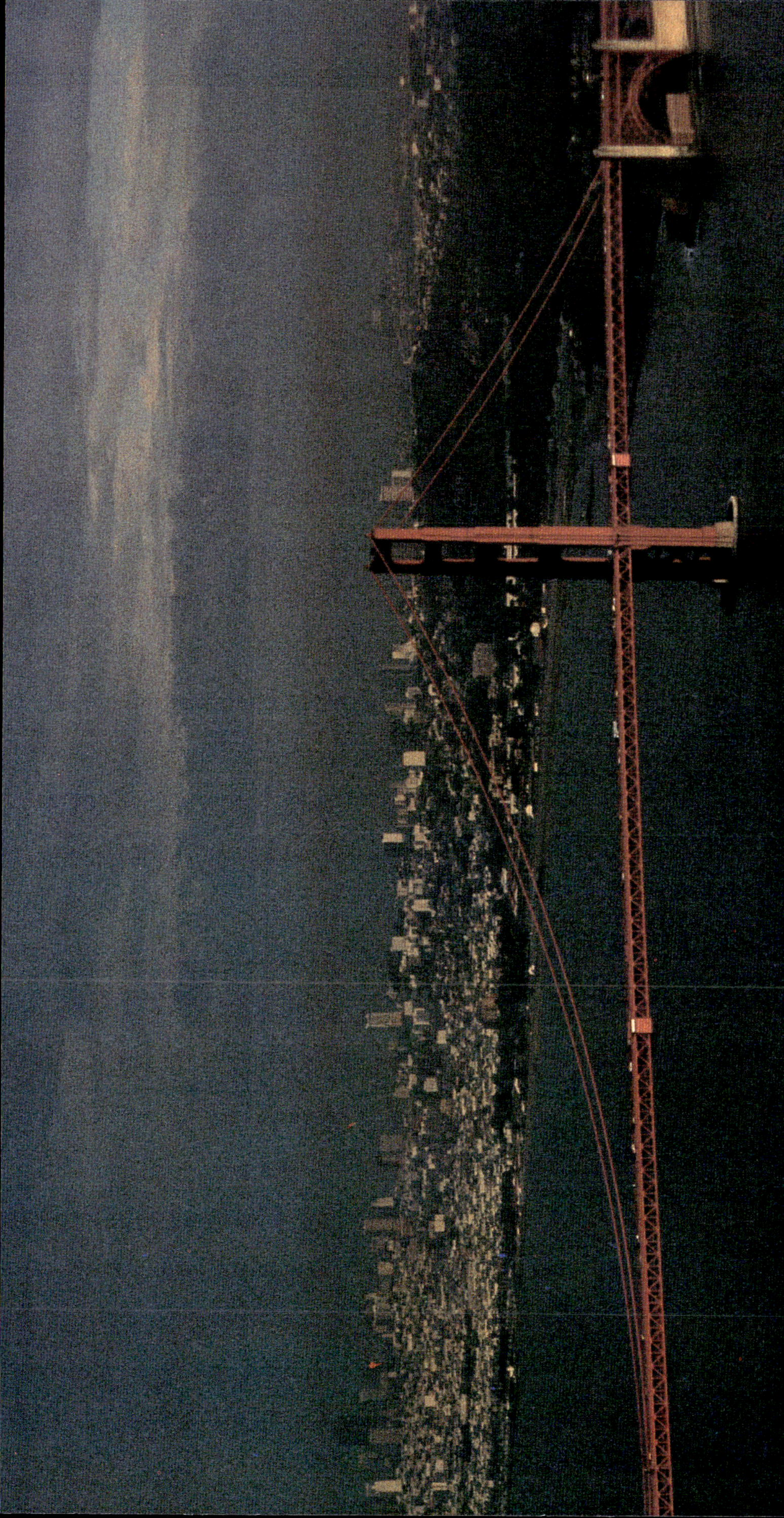

32 Across the Golden Gate you can see a host of small sailing boats crossing the strait from the relative safety of the Bay to confront the choppier waters of the Pacific.

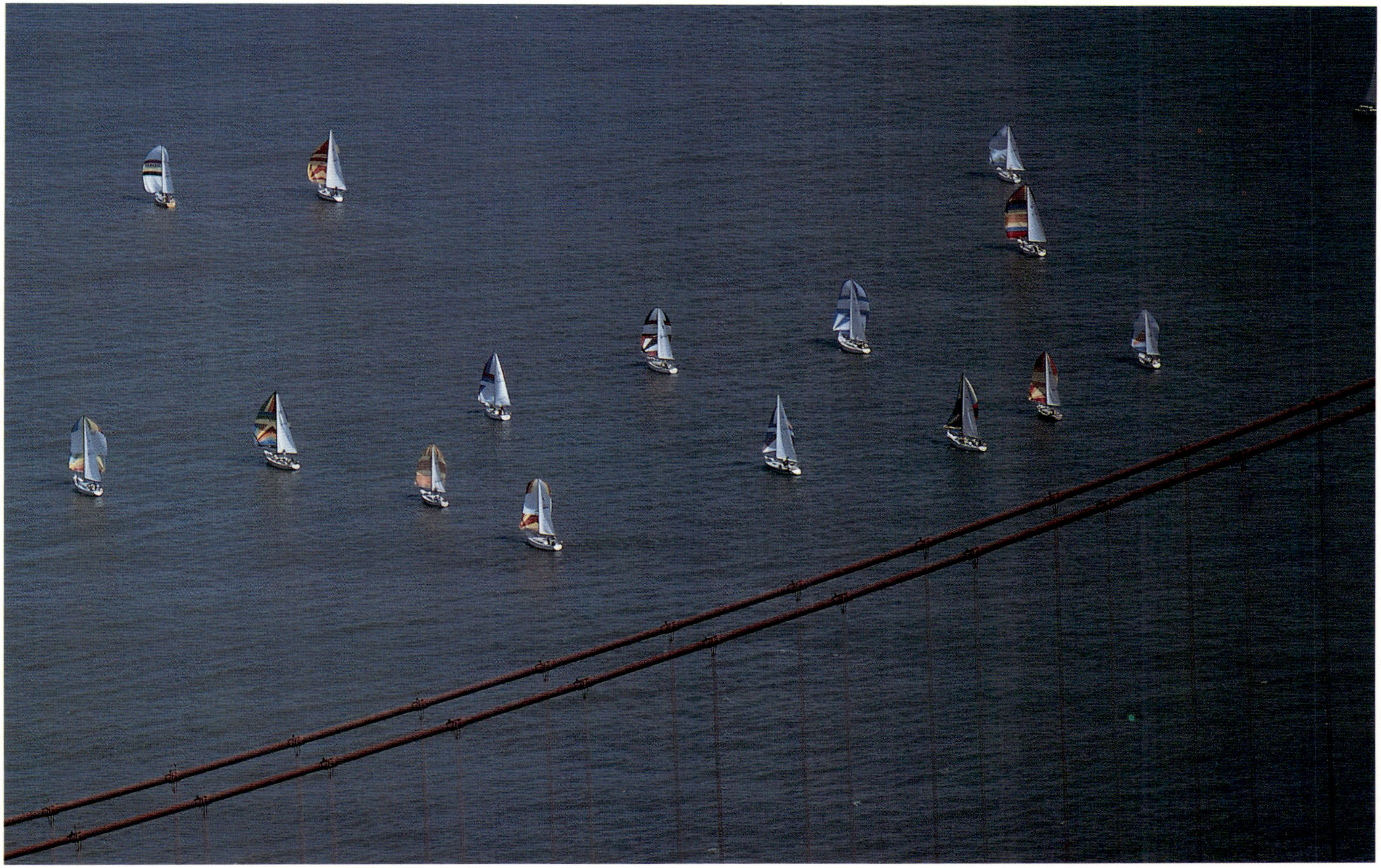

33 Sailing is a popular sport for the residents of San Francisco but even in the comparative shelter of the Bay there are strong currents for unwary sailors. The temperate marine climate makes sailing an all-round activity for the dedicated yachtsman.

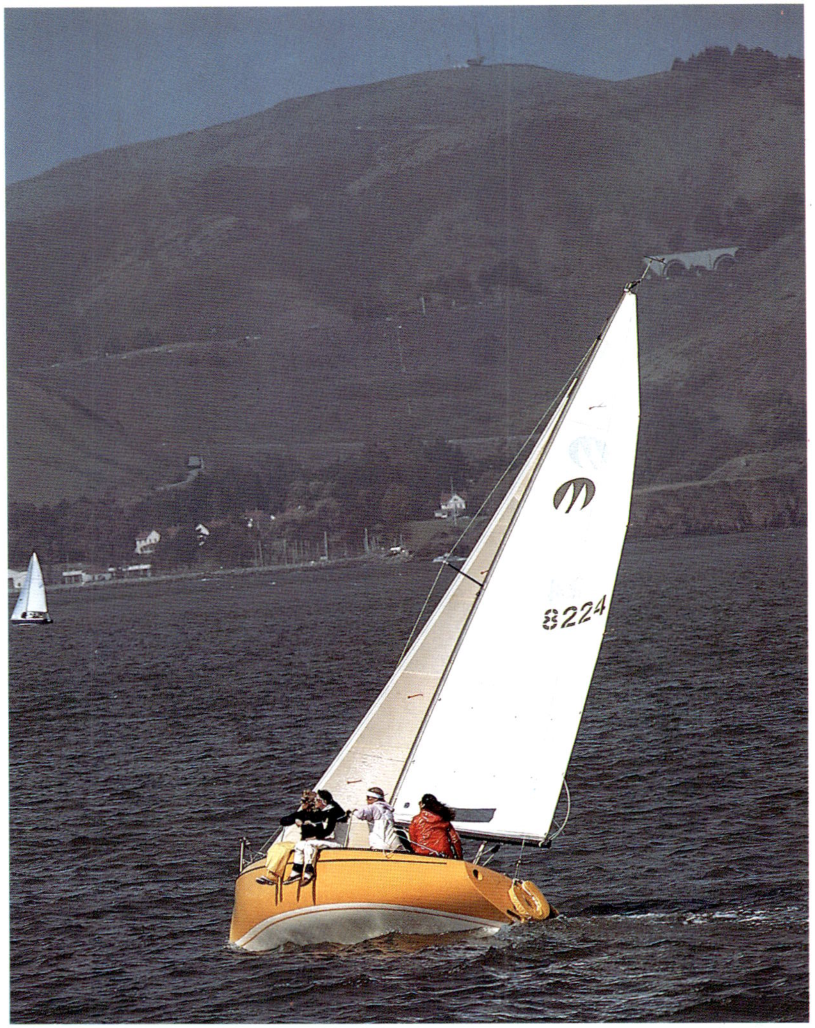

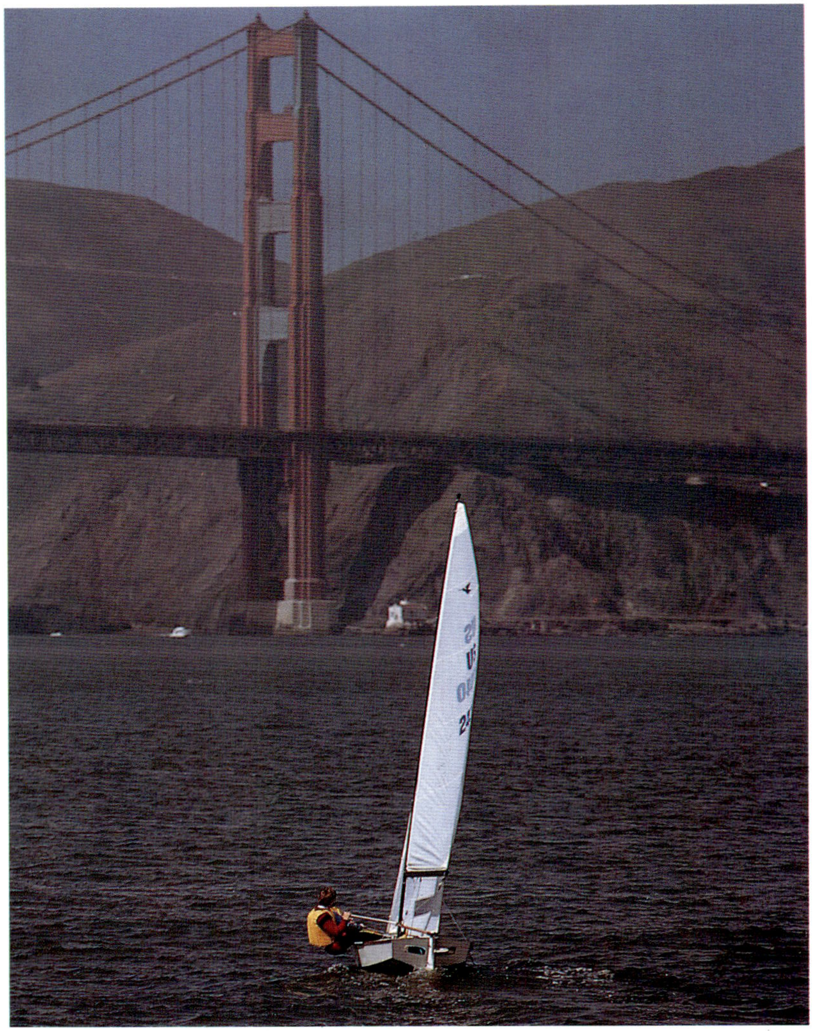

34-35 Californians are passionate devotees of sport, and running and jogging have become a national pastime for young and old. Many runners of all abilities take part in local 10K races, half-marathons and marathons. The Bay to Breakers Race in May is the most important event of all. Cycling is equally popular and many cyclists head across the Golden Gate Bridge to Marin County at weekends. There are numerous jogging routes and cycling tracks in the city's parks, most notably in Golden Gate Park.

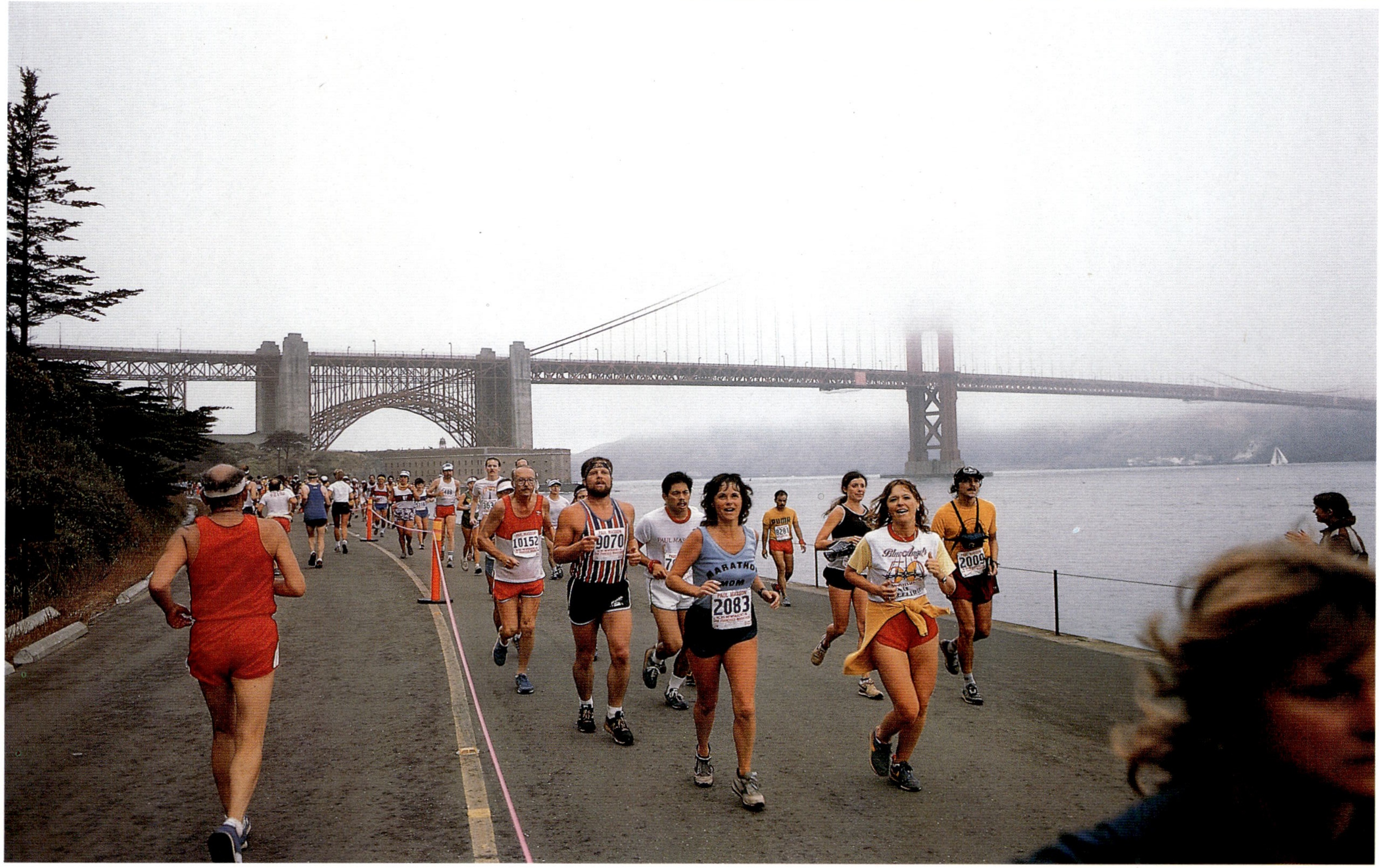

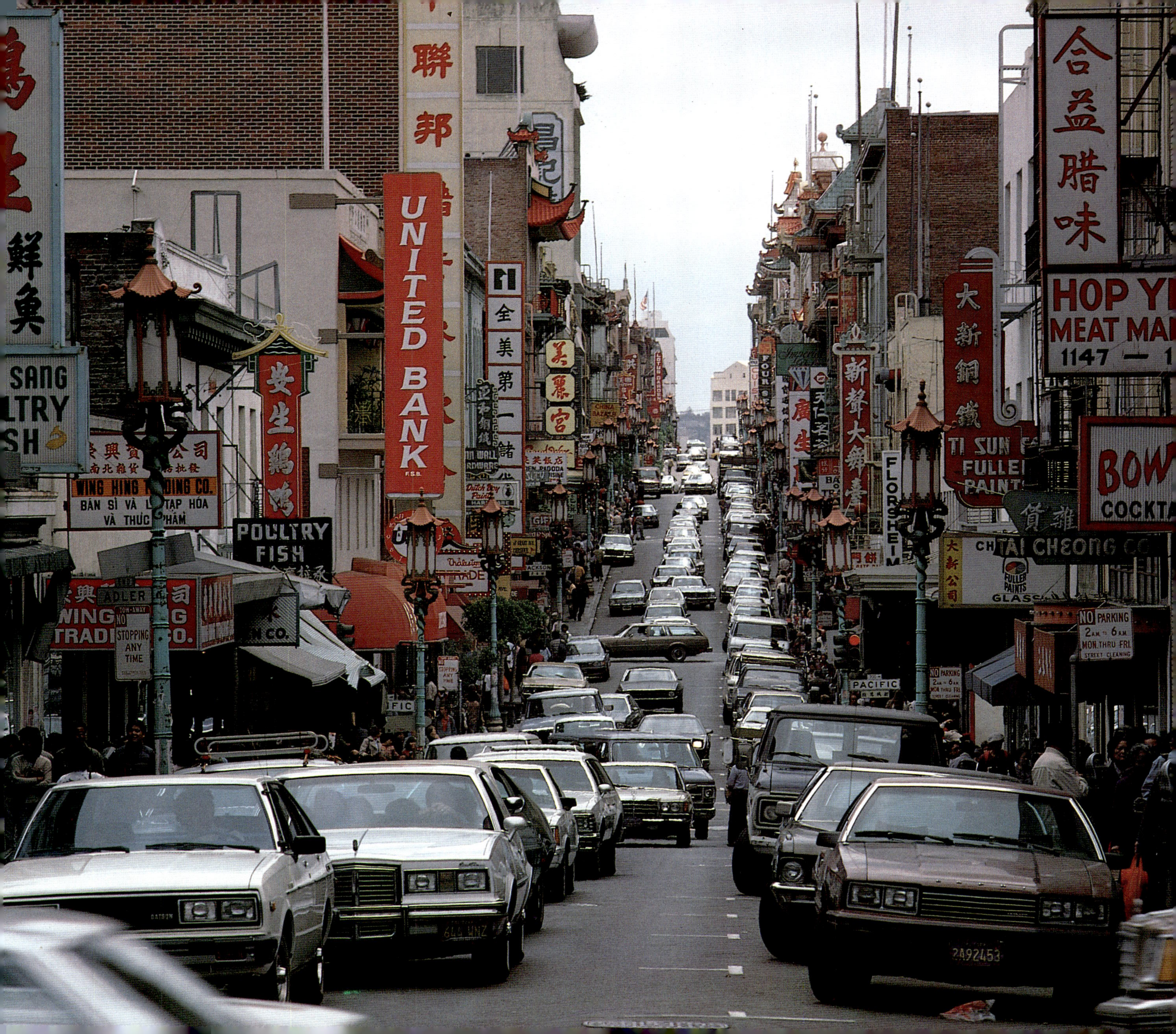
UNITED BANK
HOP YI
MEAT MA
POULTRY
FISH
TI SUN
FULLER
PAINT
WING HING TRADING CO.
BAN SI VA LE TAP HOA
VA THUC PHAM
NO PARKING
2 AM - 6 AM
MON THRU FRI
STREET CLEANING
NO STOPPING ANY TIME
PACIFIC
FLORSHEIM
合益腊味
安生鷄鴨
聯邦

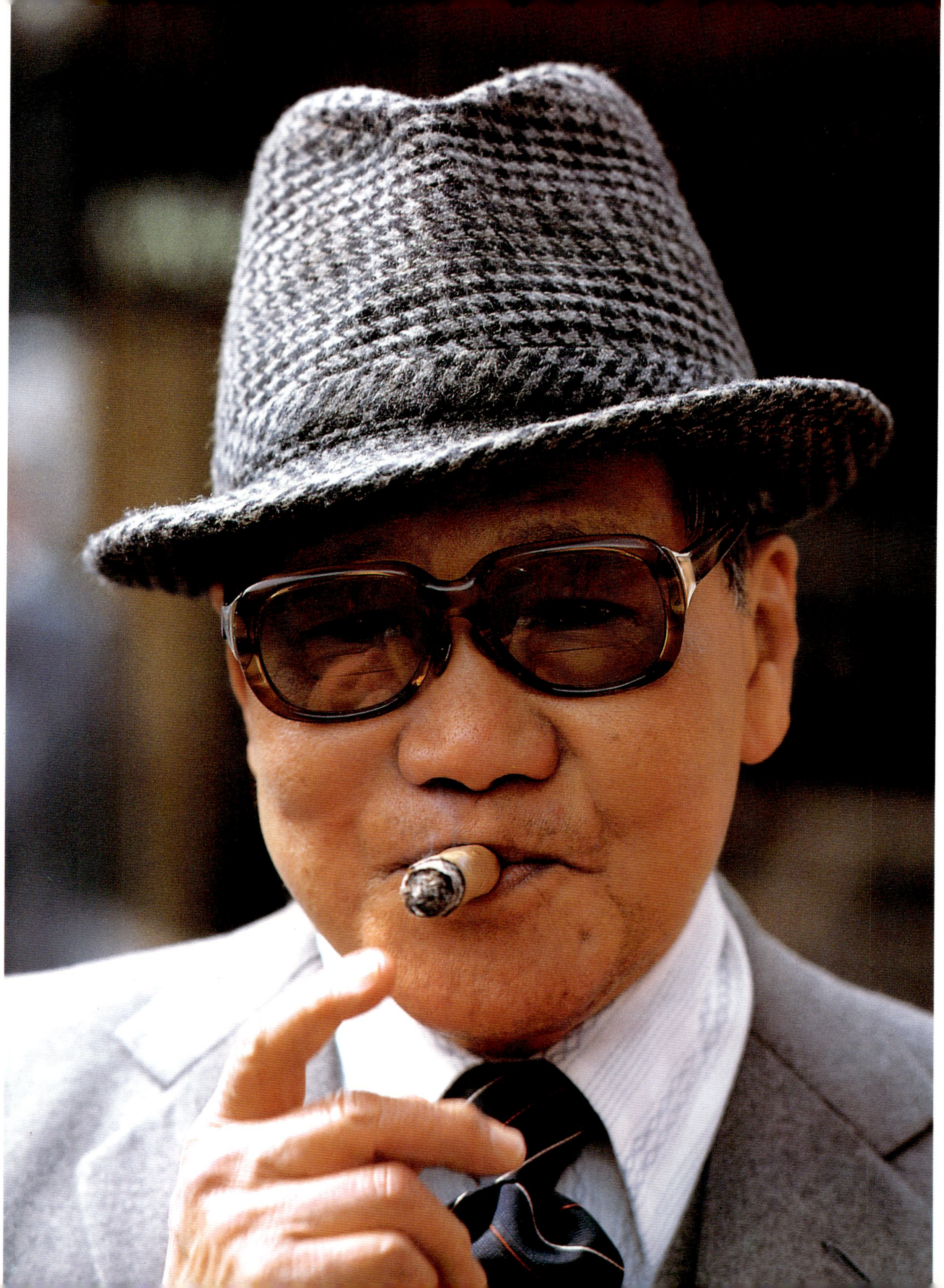

44-45 Anxious to perpetuate their customs and traditional way of life, Chinatown residents tend not to mix with other ethnic groups and continue to marry amongst themselves. However, the children attend public schools and many have acquired the American way of life while still maintaining a link with the past and the old traditions.

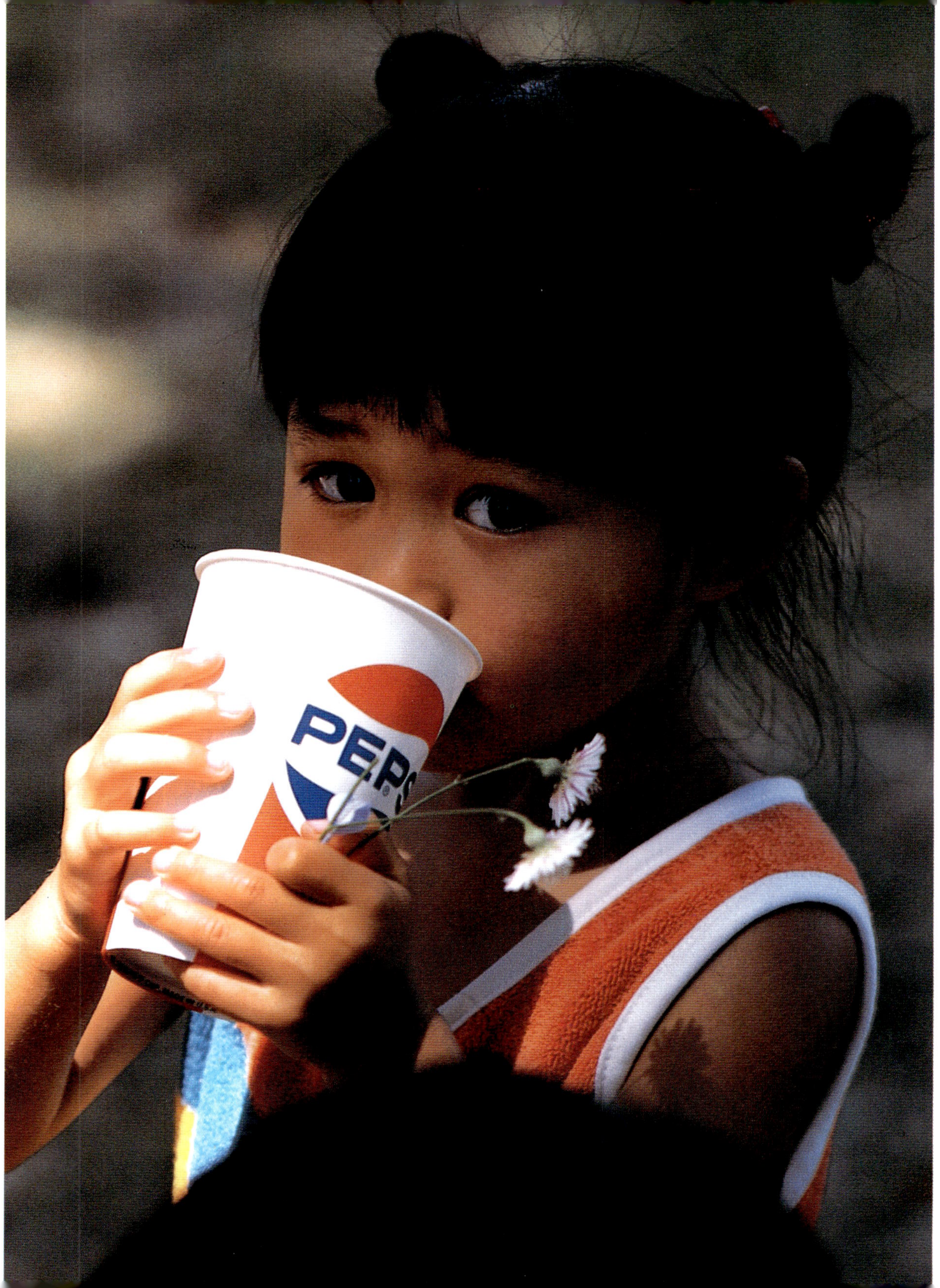

46-47 At night, Chinatown is illuminated with brightly lit neon signs proclaiming the delights of restaurants, bars, discos and nightclubs. These are mostly frequented by the Chinese, while at lunchtime the area is crowded with tourists and residents eating dim sum.

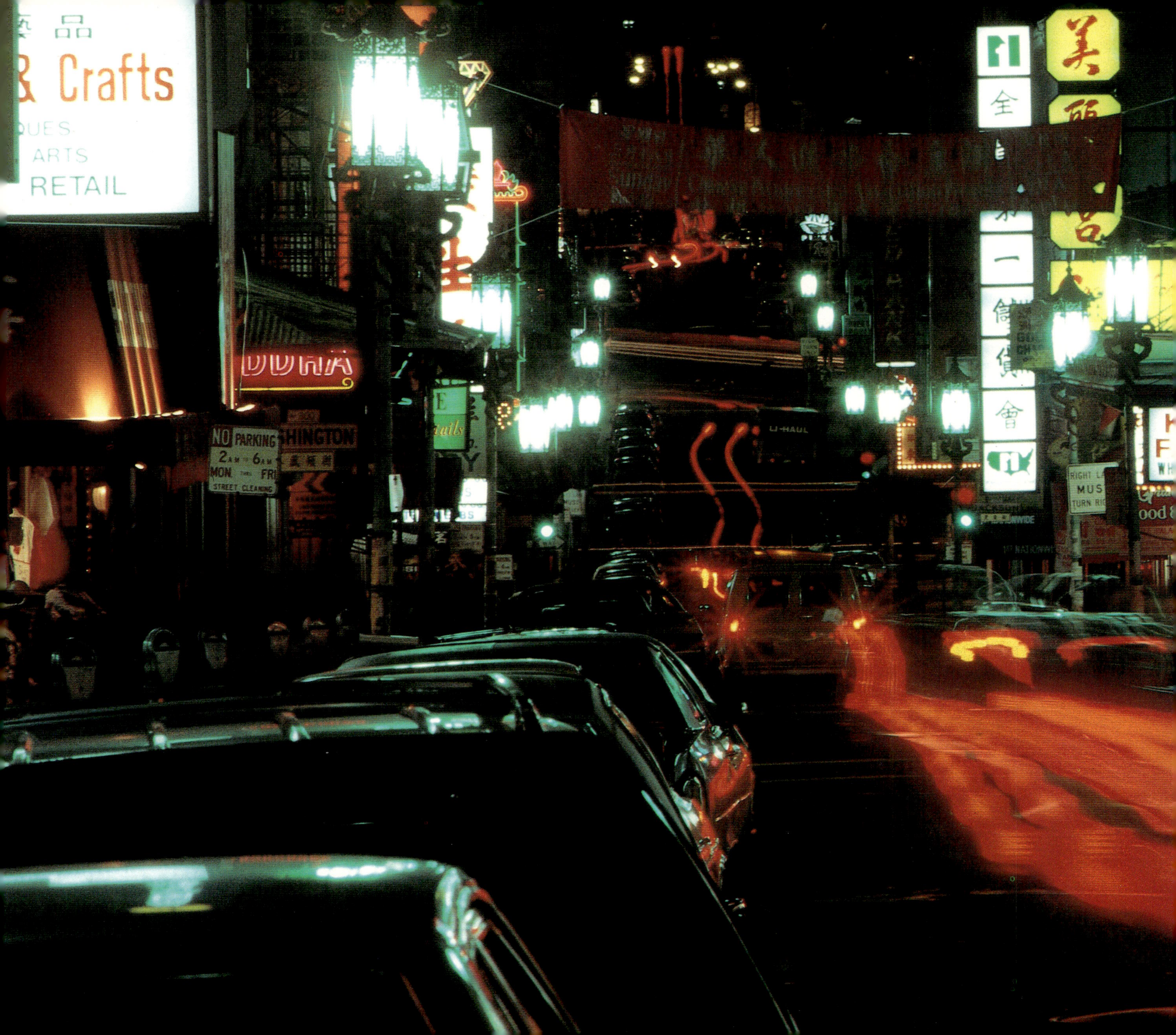
& Crafts
ARTS
RETAIL
NO PARKING
2 AM 6 AM
MON FRI
STREET CLEANING
U-HAUL

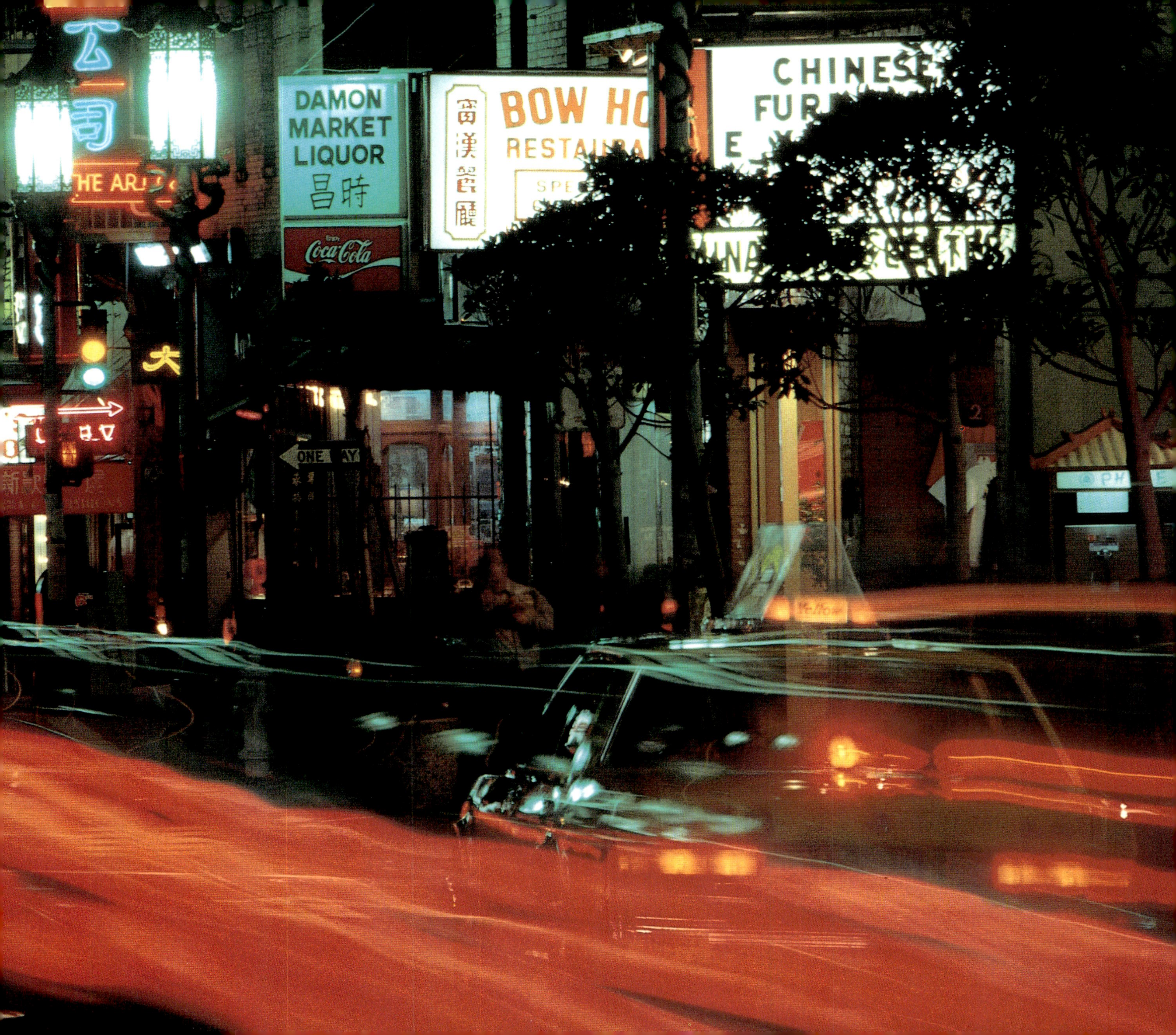
DAMON
MARKET
LIQUOR
昌時
Coca-Cola
BOW HO
RESTAU
CHINESE
ONE WAY

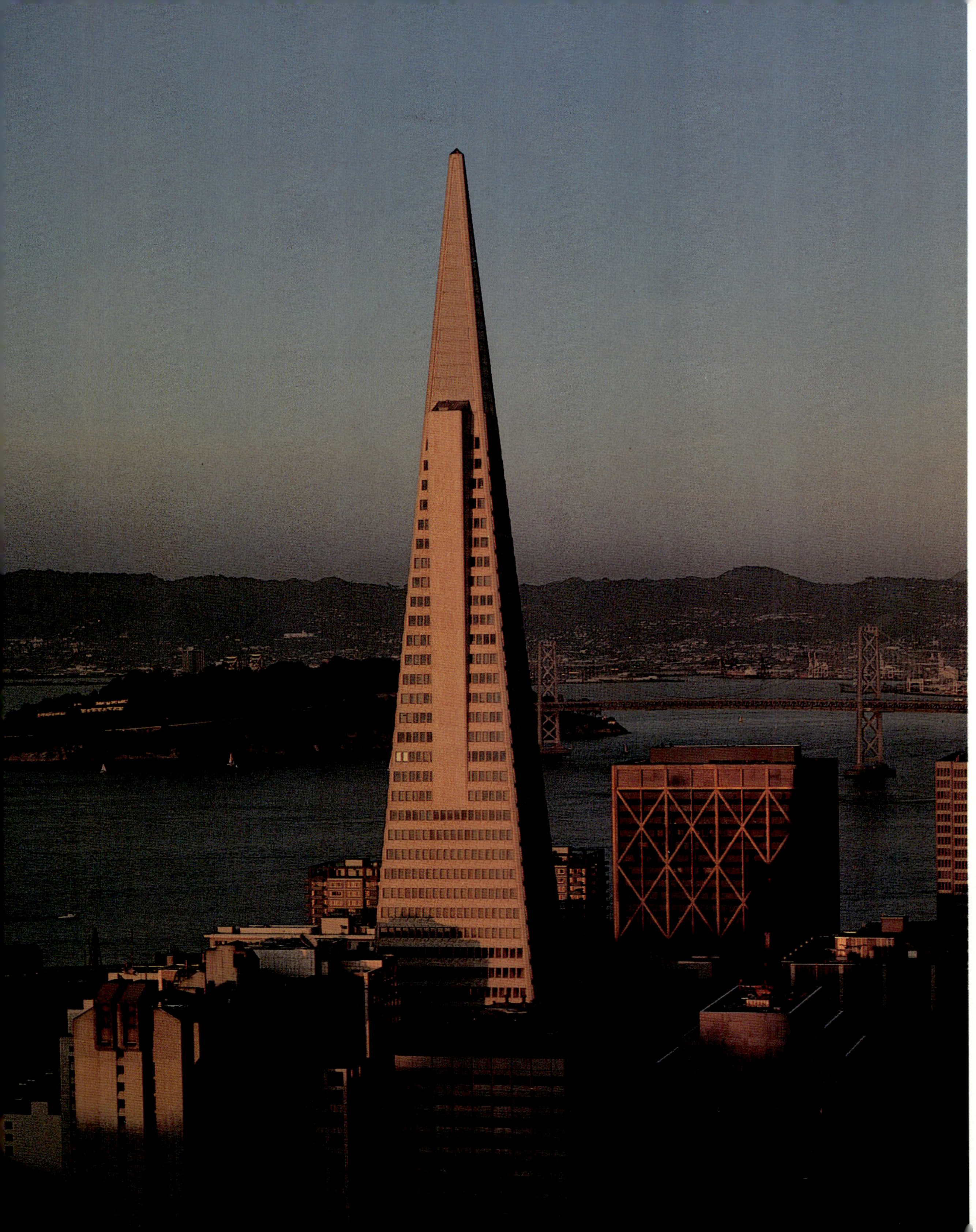

48 The futuristic pyramid structure of the Transamerica Building is highlighted by the setting sun. The tallest and most distinctive building in the city, it has attracted lavish praise and hostility from San Franciscans since it was built in 1972.

49 The Oakland Bay Bridge which was opened in 1936, is 4½ miles/7 kilometres long, and connects the commuter communities of Oakland and Berkeley with the city. Oakland has many parks, lakes and spacious homes, while leafy Berkeley has one of the finest universities in the United States.

50-51 The dazzling sunset is reflected on the glass surfaces of the downtown skyscrapers. If it was not for the Transamerica Pyramid, the skyline would be virtually indistinguishable from that of any other American big city.

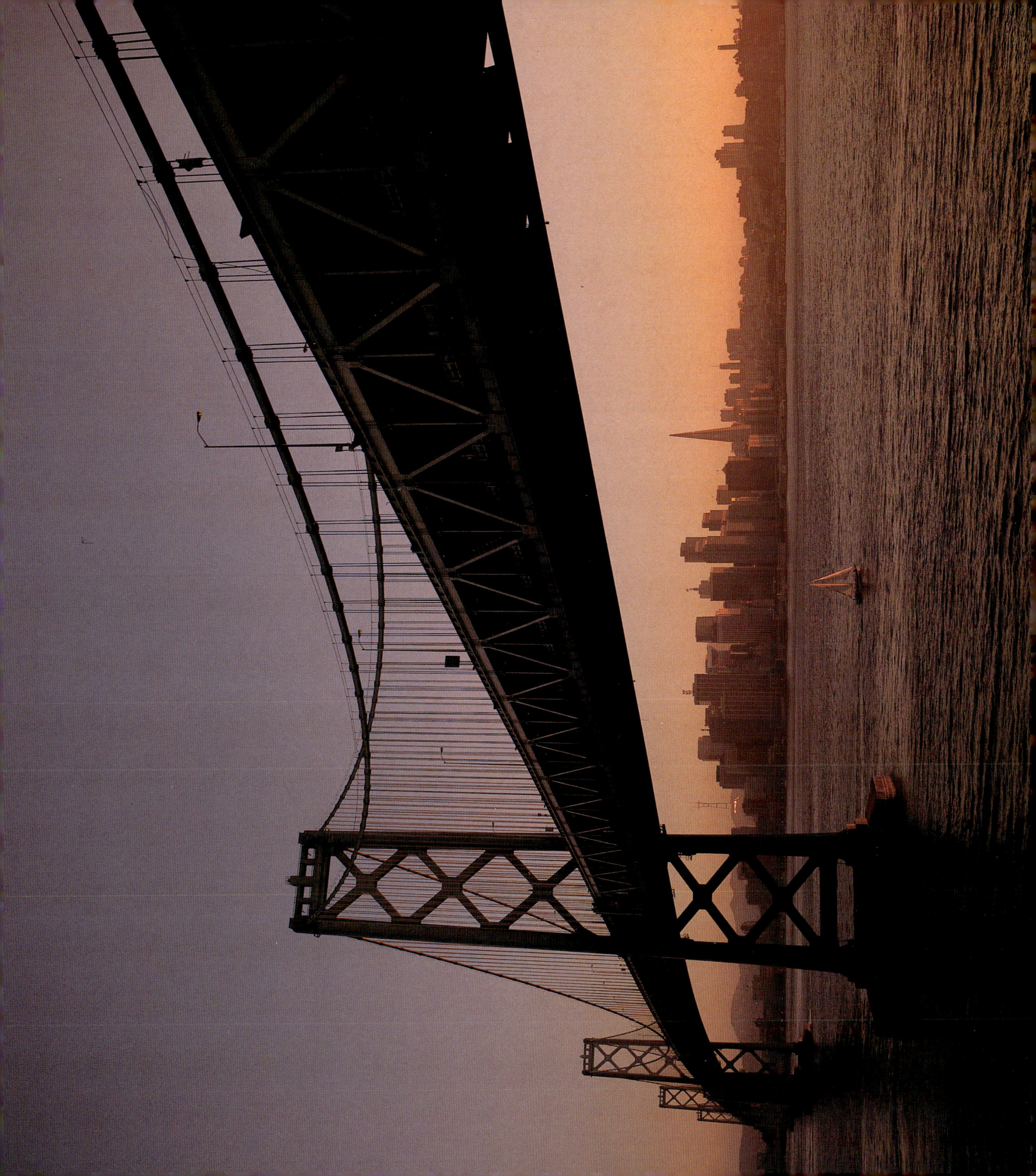

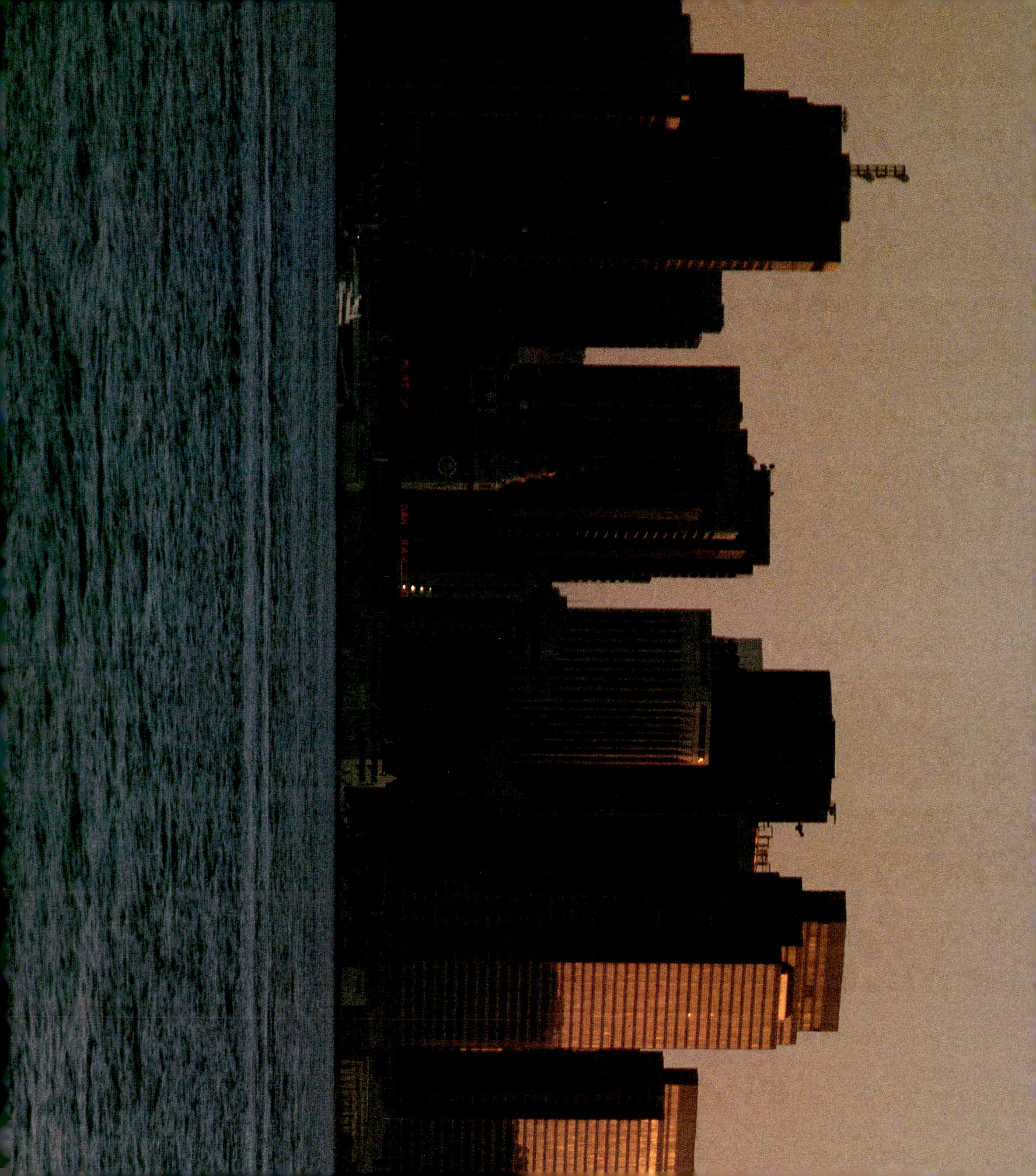

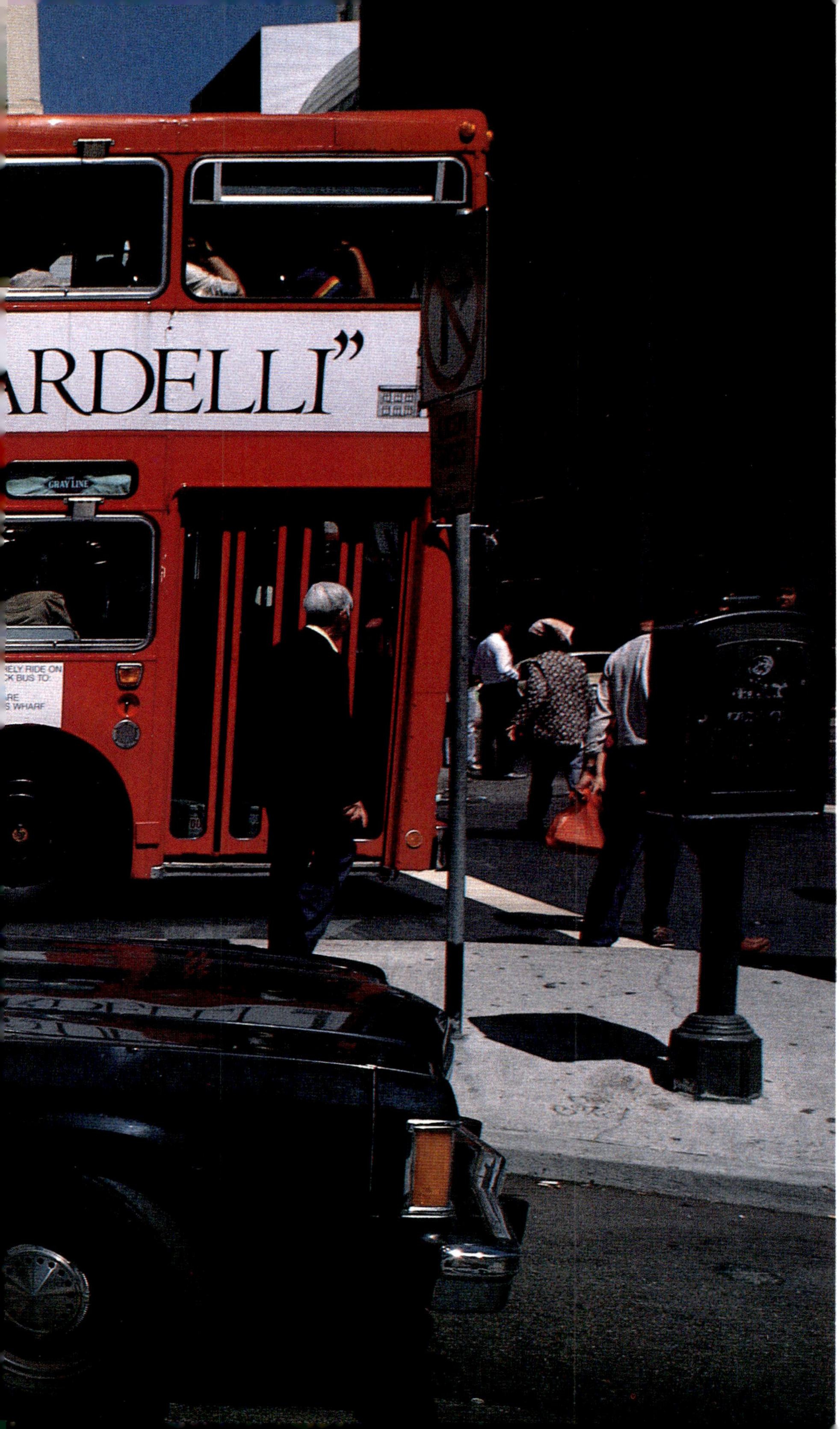

62 The famous black and white police cars and red double-decker buses are among the most popular images of San Francisco. Buses are a good and economical way to travel around the city, and you can purchase a special all-day pass which entitles you to unlimited travel.

63 Along with Montgomery Street, California Street is the financial heart of San Francisco, so much so that the area has been nicknamed the 'Wall Street' of the West Coast.

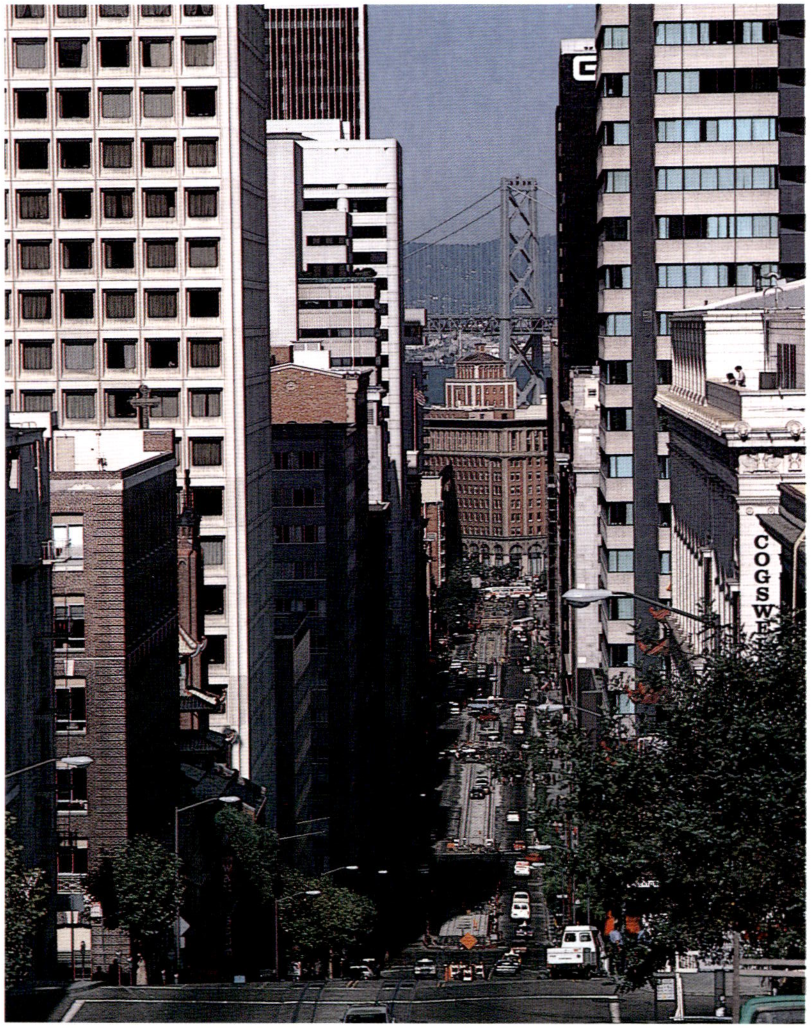

64-65 San Francisco is proud of its liberal and radical traditions and its reputation as a tolerant and free-thinking city. It has the largest gay community in the world, many of whom live in the area around Castro Street which has become a mecca for gay men and women and an important political force in the city. This is a flamboyant neighborhood which openly proclaims the homosexuality of its residents. It is estimated that about 250,000 gay people live in the city today.

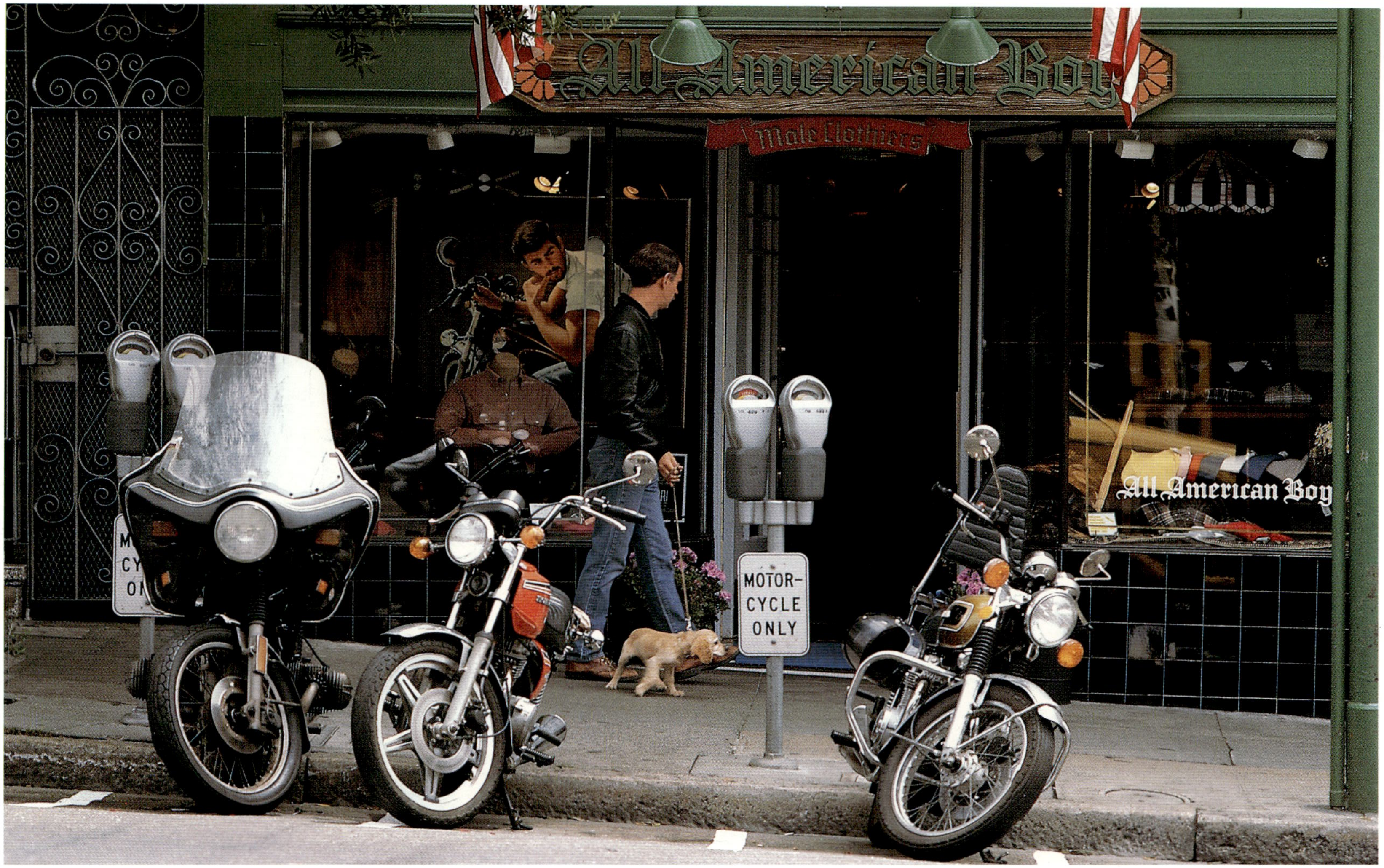

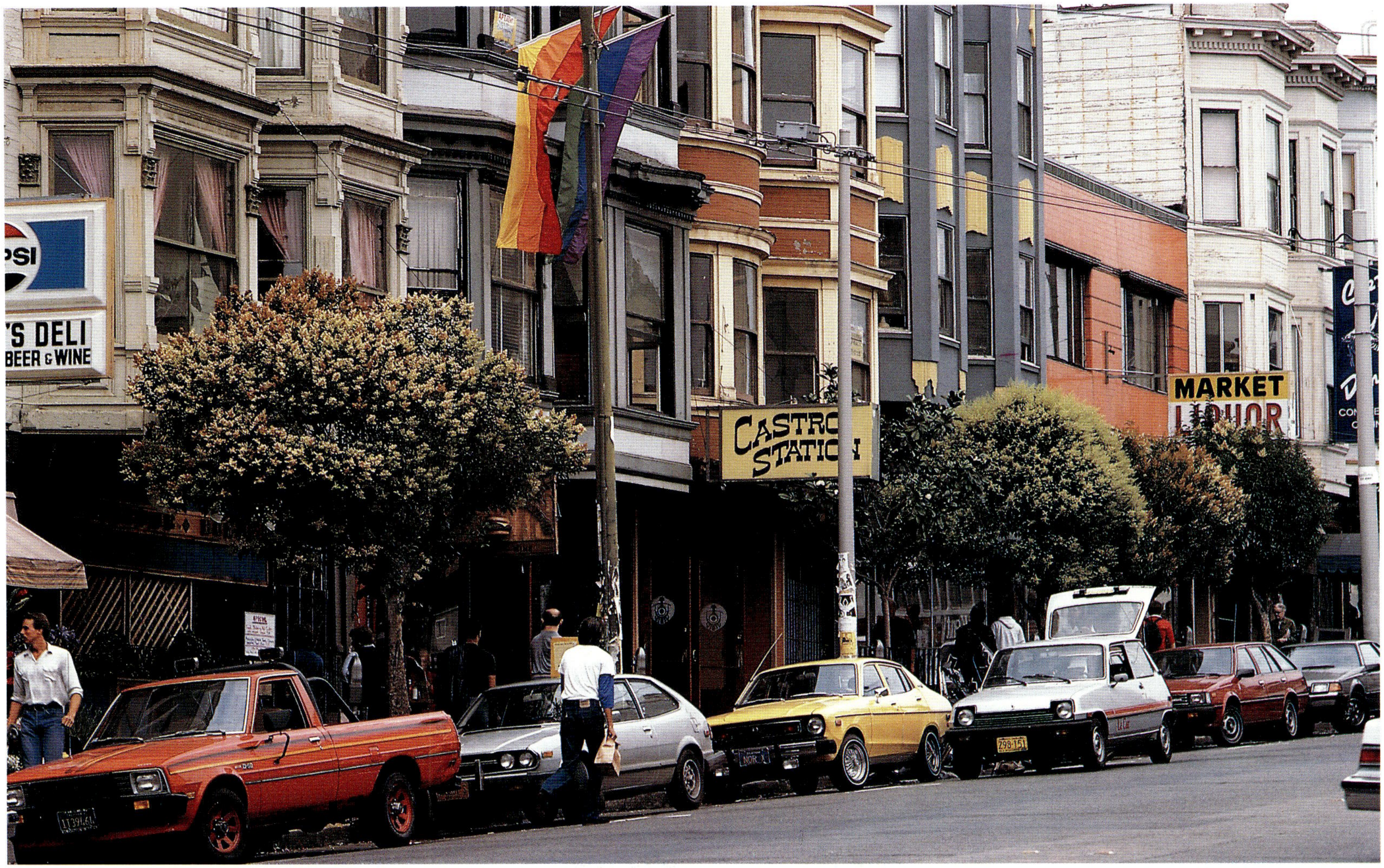
'S DELI
BEER & WINE
CASTRO
STATION
MARKET

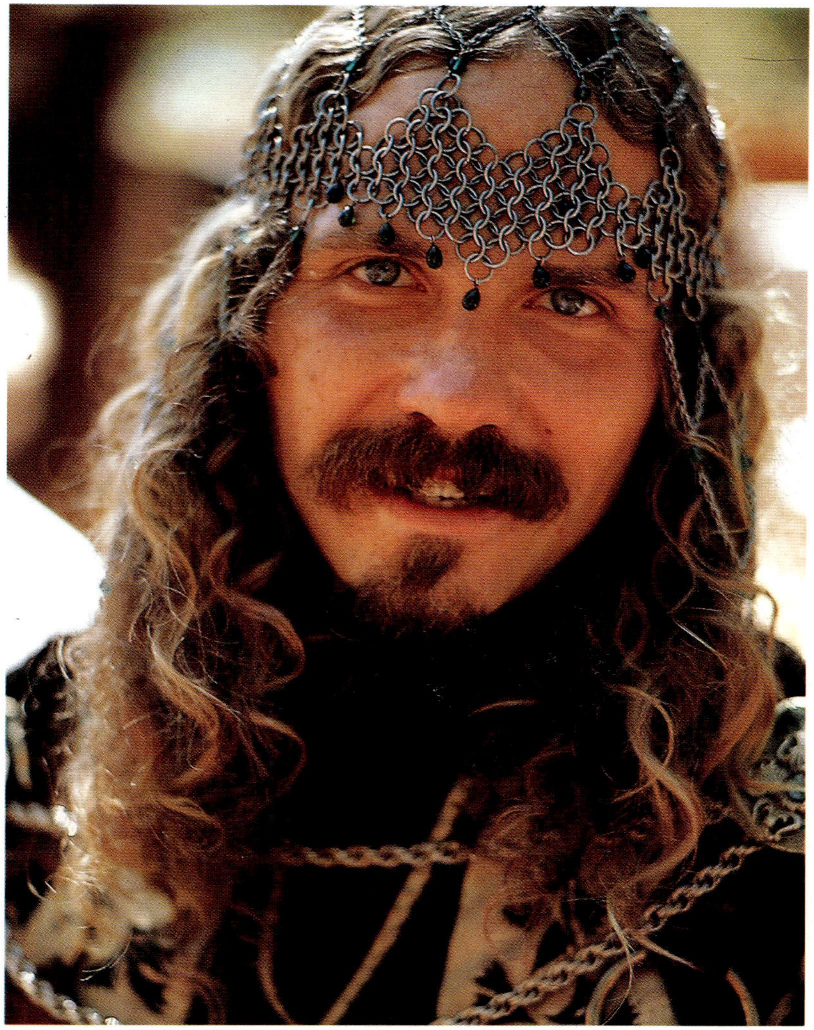

66 Every year in Marin County, a Renaissance Fair is held at which the locals dress up in elaborate costumes in the style of the Middle Ages. The festival is extremely popular and well attended by people from across the Bay as well as the locals.

Within walking distance of Union Square in the middle of the shopping district is Nob Hill with its exclusive residences. Ever since those far-off days of the Gold Rush, this has been one of the most prestigious and fashionable districts of San Francisco. It was named Nob Hill in the 1870s when four notable millionaires settled here and built sumptuous mansions on the hill. The élite of San Francisco society still lives there and it also boasts four first-class hotels. At the top of the hill is the exclusive Pacific Union Club which is housed in one of the original mansions which survived the earthquake and fire of 1906. In the same area, you can visit the old cable car depot, Cable Car's Barn, which is now a museum with scale models of the early cable cars, archive material and memorabilia.

San Francisco has a wide range of museums, and inside Golden Gate Park there are three: the M. H. de Young Memorial Museum, the Asian Art Museum which is famous for its jade and porcelain collections, and the California Academy of Sciences which houses a planetarium and an aquarium. Most notable for its fine collection of contemporary art is the Museum of Modern Art, on the west side of City Hall, with its displays of works by Klee, Pollock and Calder, Matisse and other twentieth-century artists. There are also some more unusual museums, this being San Francisco, such as the Mexican Museum near Fort Mason which features Mexican folk art, and the elegant Wine Museum bequeathed by the Christian Brothers. Even stranger is the Wax Museum in Chinatown which records memorable events in Chinese history, and the Guinness Book of World Records Museum in Fisherman's Wharf, and the crazy Ripley's Believe It or Not Museum which is

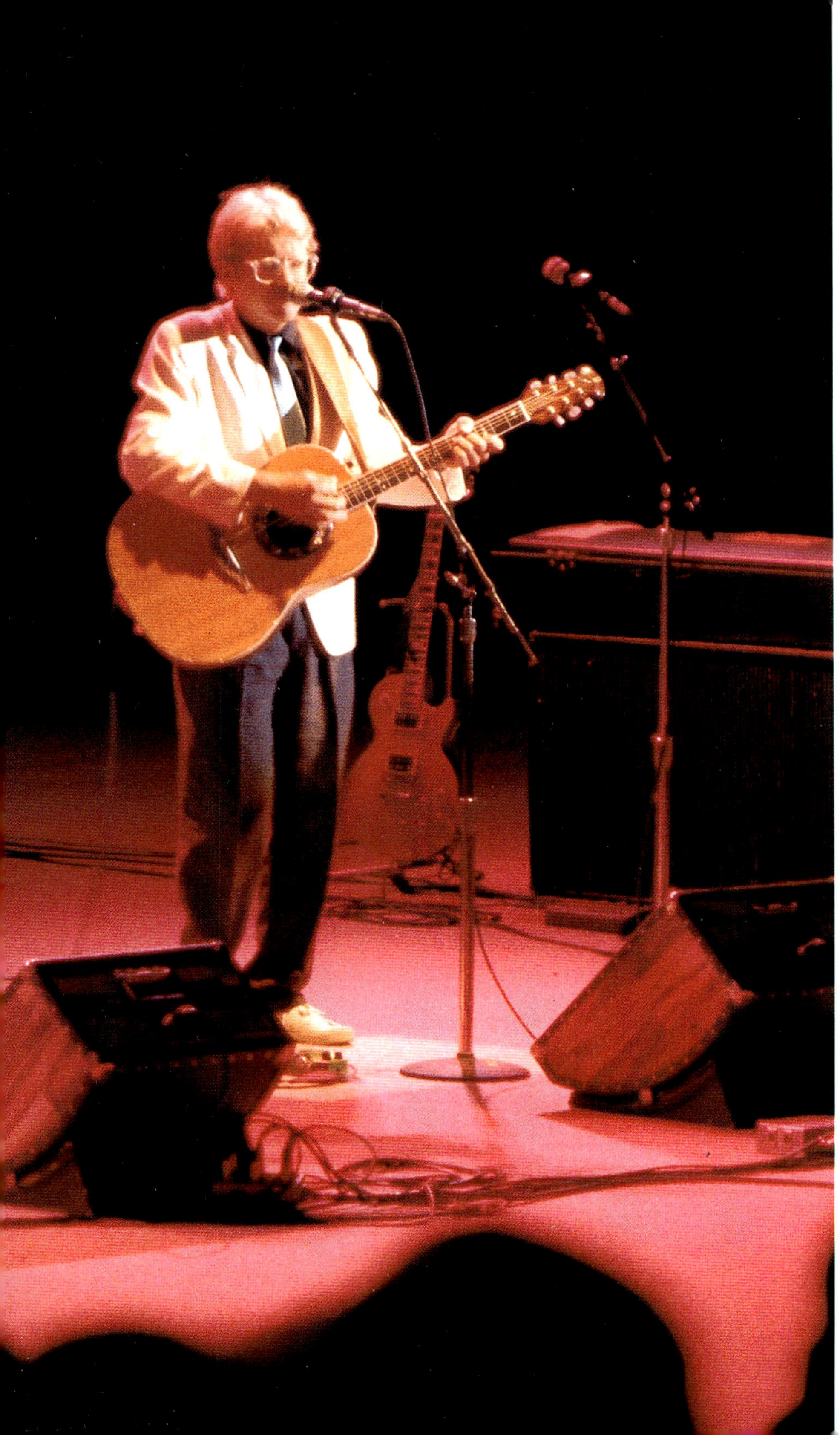

68-69 Live music of every kind is popular in the clubs and nightspots of the city. Rock, jazz, blues, country and western, folk and even big band music are all part of San Francisco's rich nightlife.

devoted to the mysterious and the absurd. San Francisco is a center for the arts and theater is very popular and of an extremely high standard. Throughout the year the Art Deco Orpheum Theater reruns Broadway shows, while at the Geary Theater, one of the best repertory companies in the States, the American Conservatory Theater, stages plays, both old and new. The city has its own symphony orchestra with a permanent home at the Davis Symphony Hall, and one of the best opera houses in the world which regularly attracts the top international stars like Luciano Pavarotti and Kiri Te Kanawa.

Music is an intrinsic part of San Francisco life, and there are countless clubs specializing in jazz, country and western, folk, rock and South American music, where well-known singers and artists often perform. In many relatively unknown clubs, it is still not unusual to see stars performing under pseudonyms. San Francisco has a varied and rich nightlife and is able to satisfy every musical taste. Along Broadway Avenue are the most conspicuous nightspots, although not necessarily the best ones. There are numerous clubs, discotheques, bars and restaurants with live music, ranging from sophisticated cabaret shows and plush piano bars to famous jazz clubs, comedy clubs and even singles bars and gay bars. San Francisco is renowned throughout the United States as a center for the arts and culture. Whether your great love is grand opera, classical music, jazz piano or rhythm and blues; whether you enjoy musicals, classical theater or more contemporary fringe shows, there is always something for everyone in this exciting city.

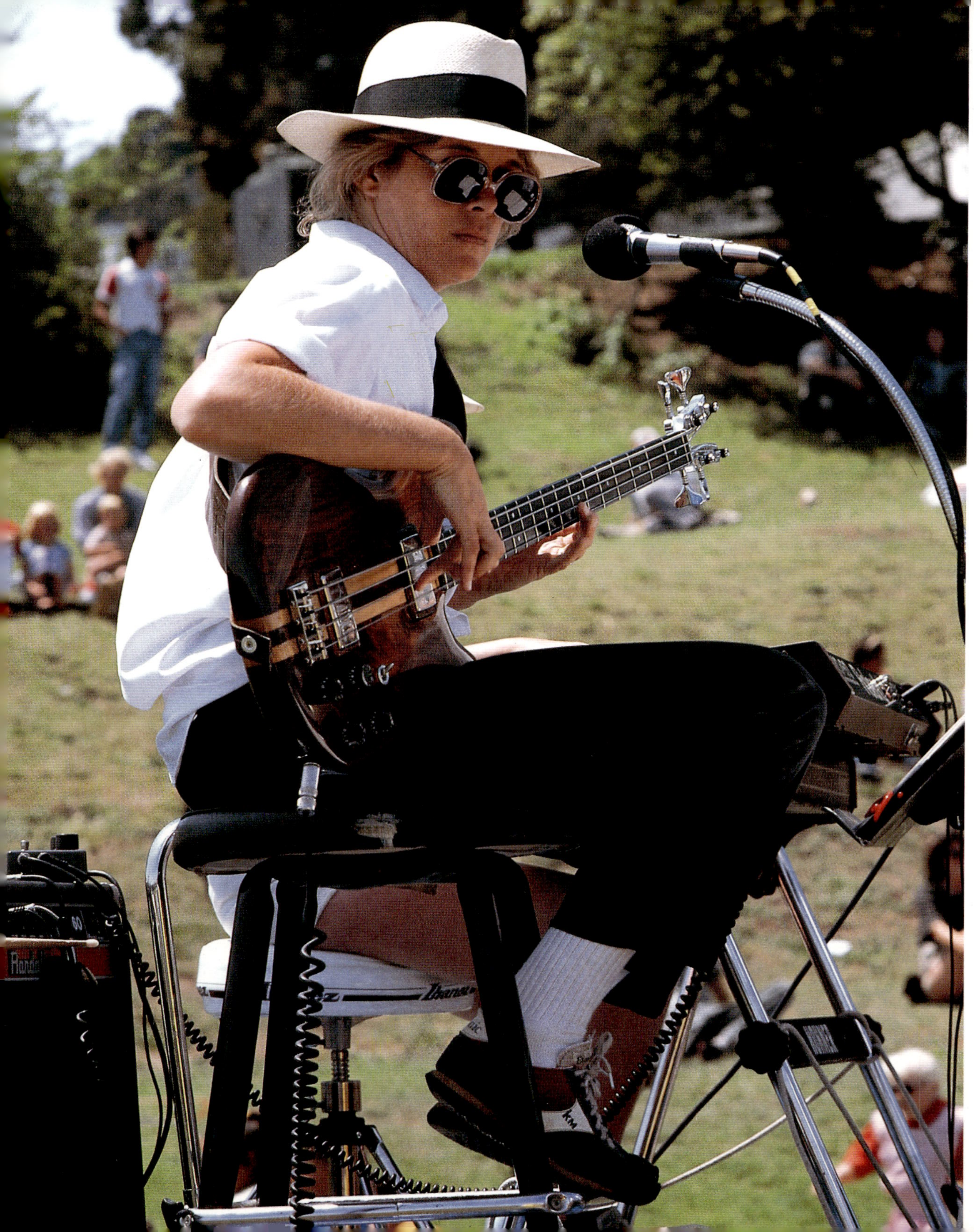

70 Buskers can be found in many of the city's streets, squares and parks, entertaining the passers-by. The traditions of American folk singing and the legacy of the Hippie culture of the 1960s are perpetuated by many of these street musicians.

71 Union Square is dressed with hundreds of green and white balloons for the annual Saint Patrick's Day celebrations and parade through the downtown area. They are traditionally held on the Sunday closest to 17 March.

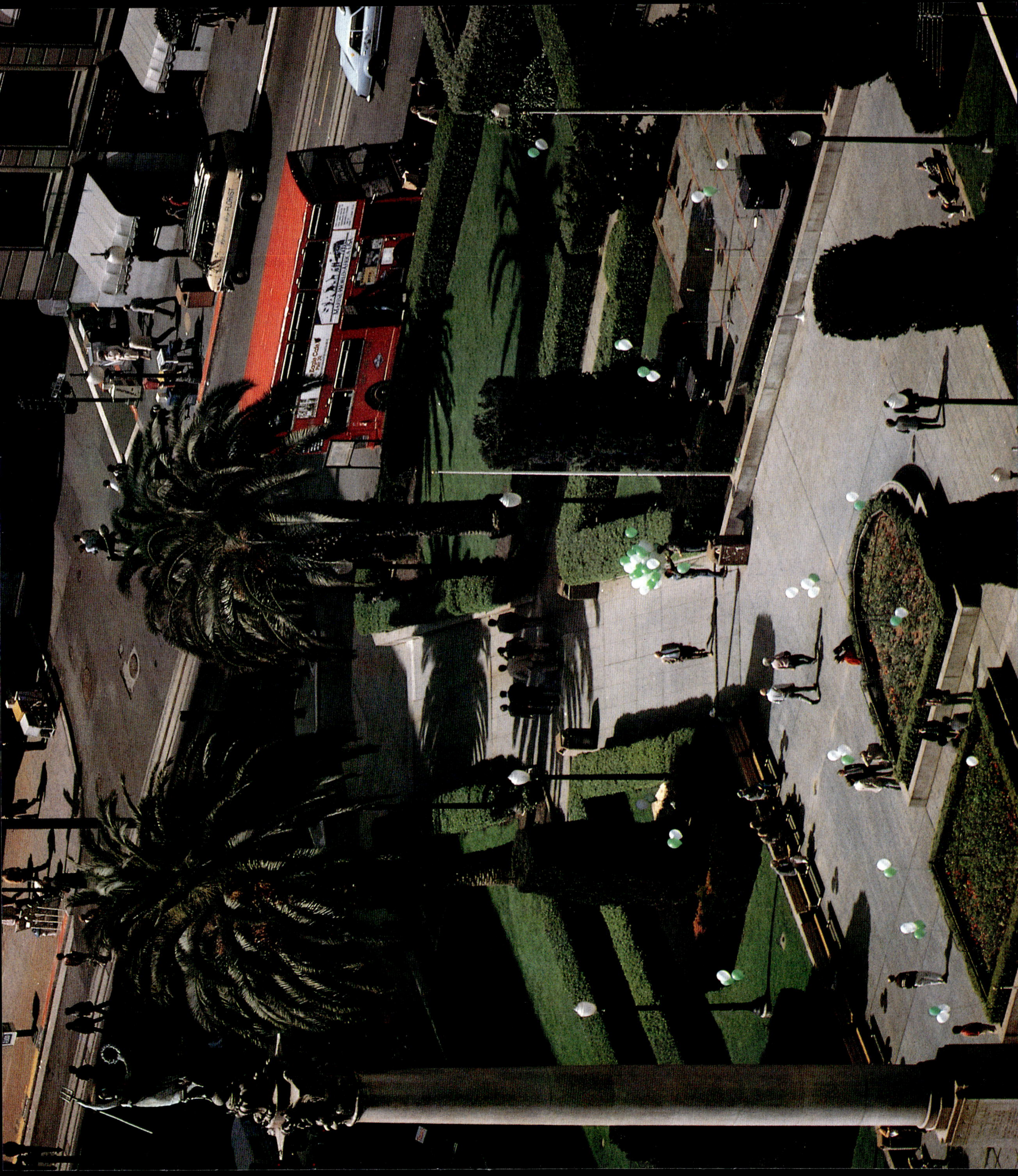

72-73 On the feast day of Saint Patrick, patron saint of the Irish, even the cable cars are adorned with green ribbons and decorations, and people wear green and white clothing and costumes.

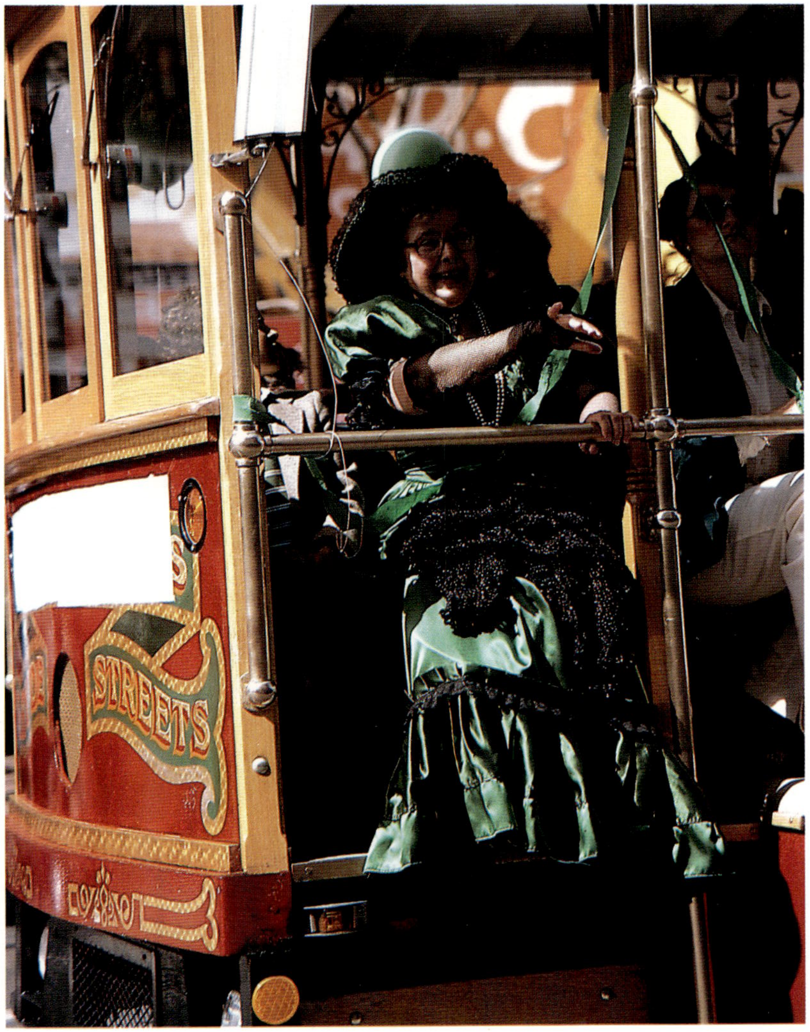

Even by day, you can be entertained by live music in the city, especially in the summer months when open-air concerts are held. On Sunday afternoons there are free band concerts in Golden Gate Park, while a free summer musical festival is staged in the Stern Grove amphitheater with musical offerings of opera, ballet, jazz, symphonic and popular music. Sports enthusiasts can watch the San Francisco 49ers playing at the vast Candlestick Park Stadium, or baseball with the San Francisco Giants. The city is a paradise for lovers of sport and the magnificent great outdoors. In Golden Gate Park, you can go jogging, visit the zoo, stroll through the brightly colored flower gardens or take tea in the exotic Japanese Tea Garden. The Botanical Gardens have more than 5000 species of flowers, while the neighboring Spreckels Lake is a favorite spot for ornithologists who gather to watch the large numbers of migratory birds. In fact, the park is much more than just an enormous public recreation area. Acquired by the city in 1868, it has become an institution – the green lungs of San Francisco and the meeting-place for thousands of its residents. There is an arboretum, a Chinese pavilion, a Dutch windmill, a tulip garden, a Shakespeare garden, an elaborate Victorian conservatory and several museums. There are also numerous paths designated specifically for cyclists and runners. One bike route runs right through the park to Lake Merced. There are also twenty-one public tennis courts and a pitch-and-putt nine-hole golf course. Whatever your particular sport or leisure interest is, you are sure to find it in San Francisco. There are gyms and fitness clubs, four public golf courses, ice rinks, sailing, tennis courts and horse riding.

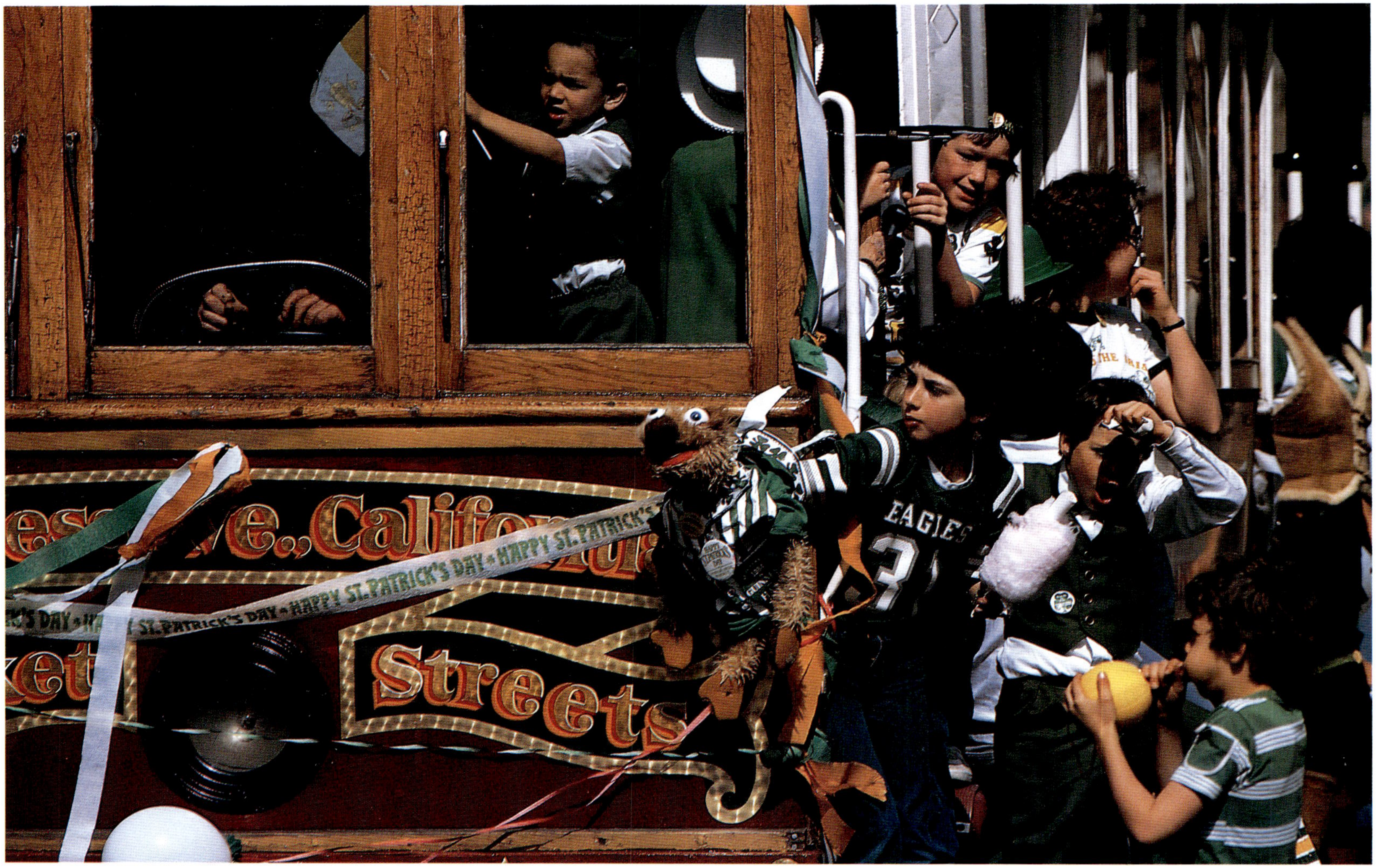

Streets
HAPPY ST. PATRICK'S DAY
EAGLES

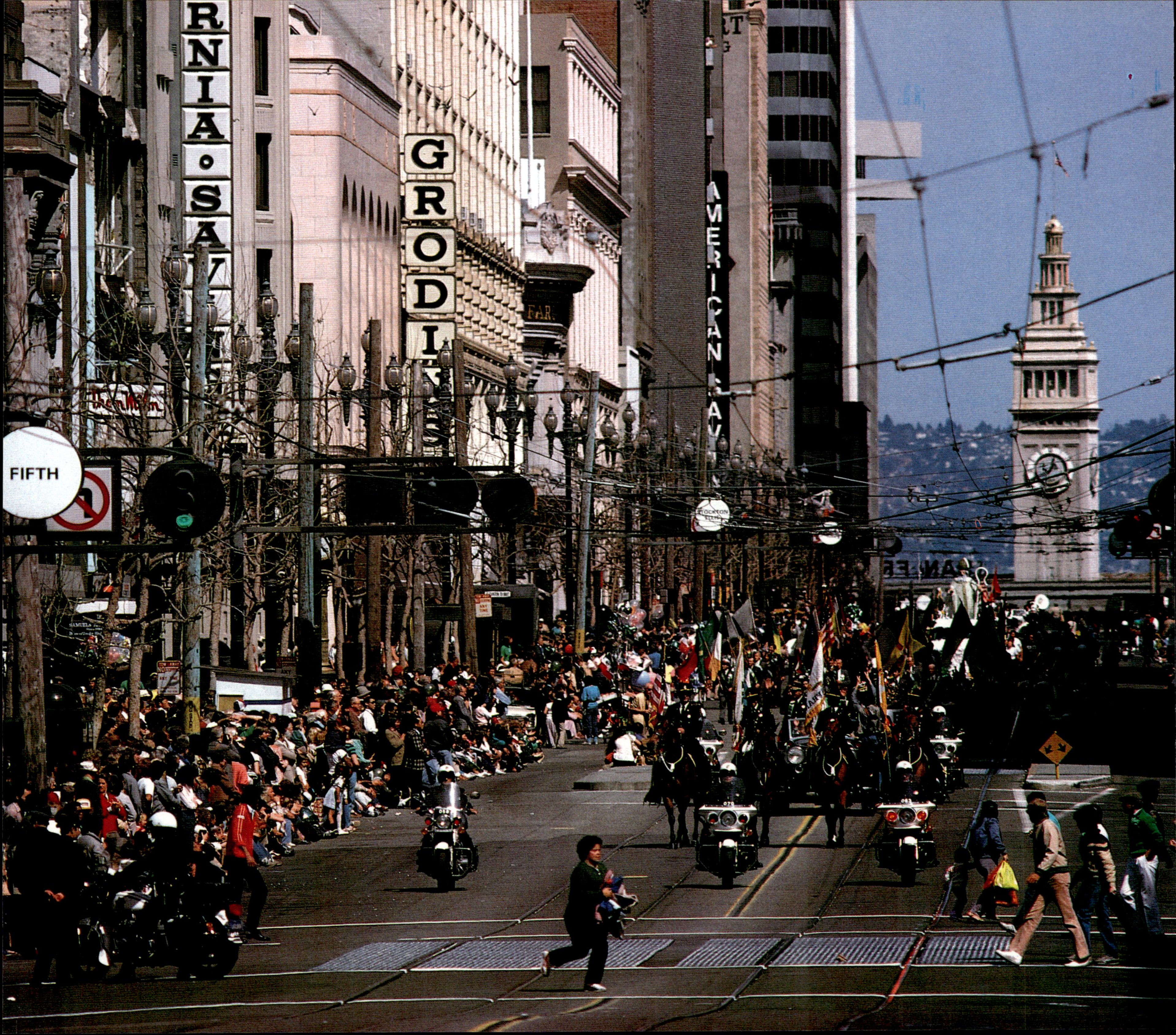
FIFTH
GRODINS
AMERICAN

74-75 On Saint Patrick's Day, all regular traffic is diverted well away from Market Street where the colorful parade is staged. A statue of the saint is carried in the procession, adorned with white carnations some of which are dyed orange and green specially for the occasion to emulate the colors of the Irish tricolor flag.

76-77 Many children, some of Irish origin, watch the annual Saint Patrick's Day parade pass by and join in the festivities.

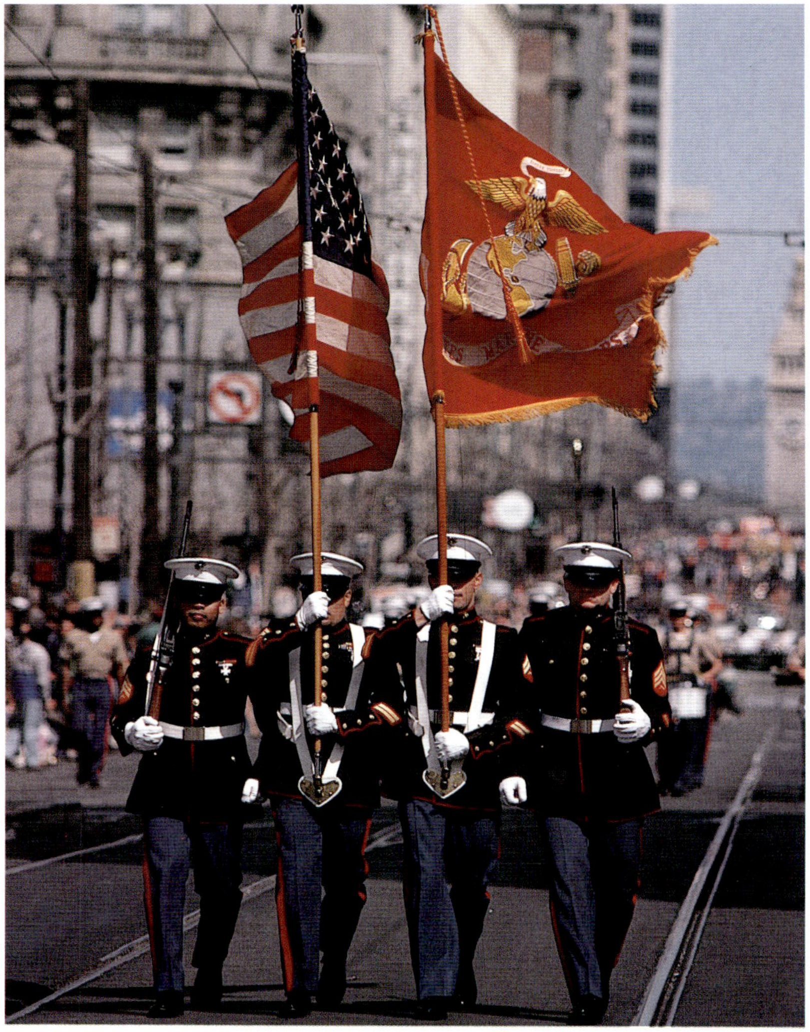

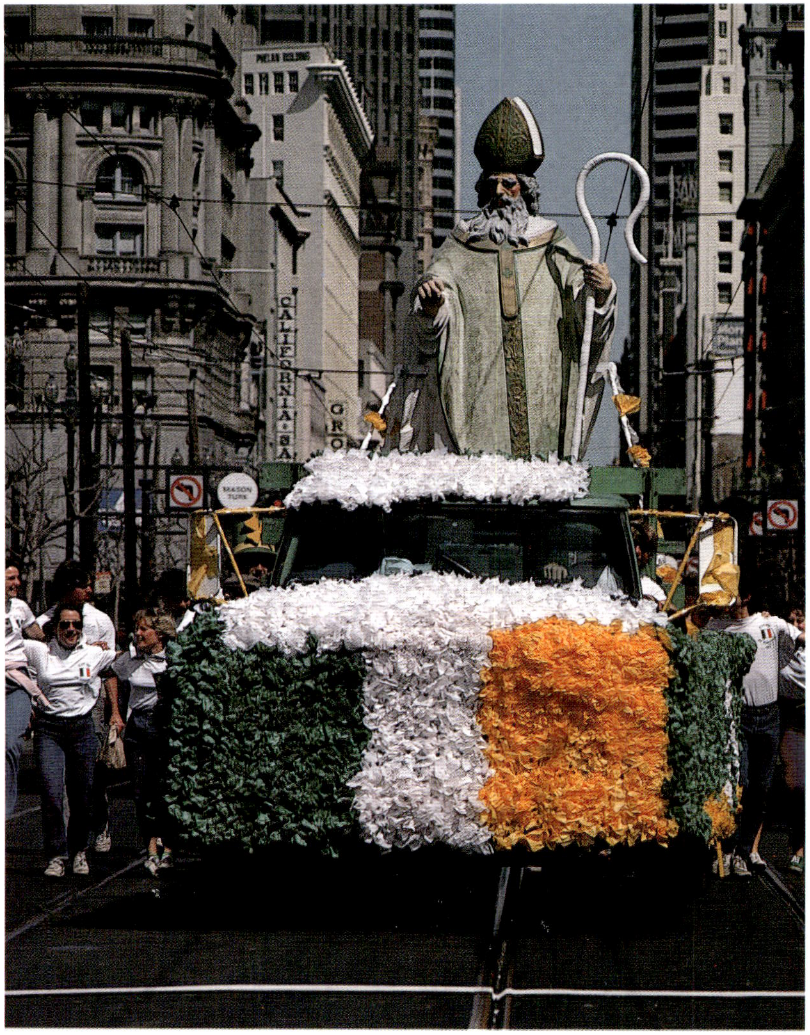

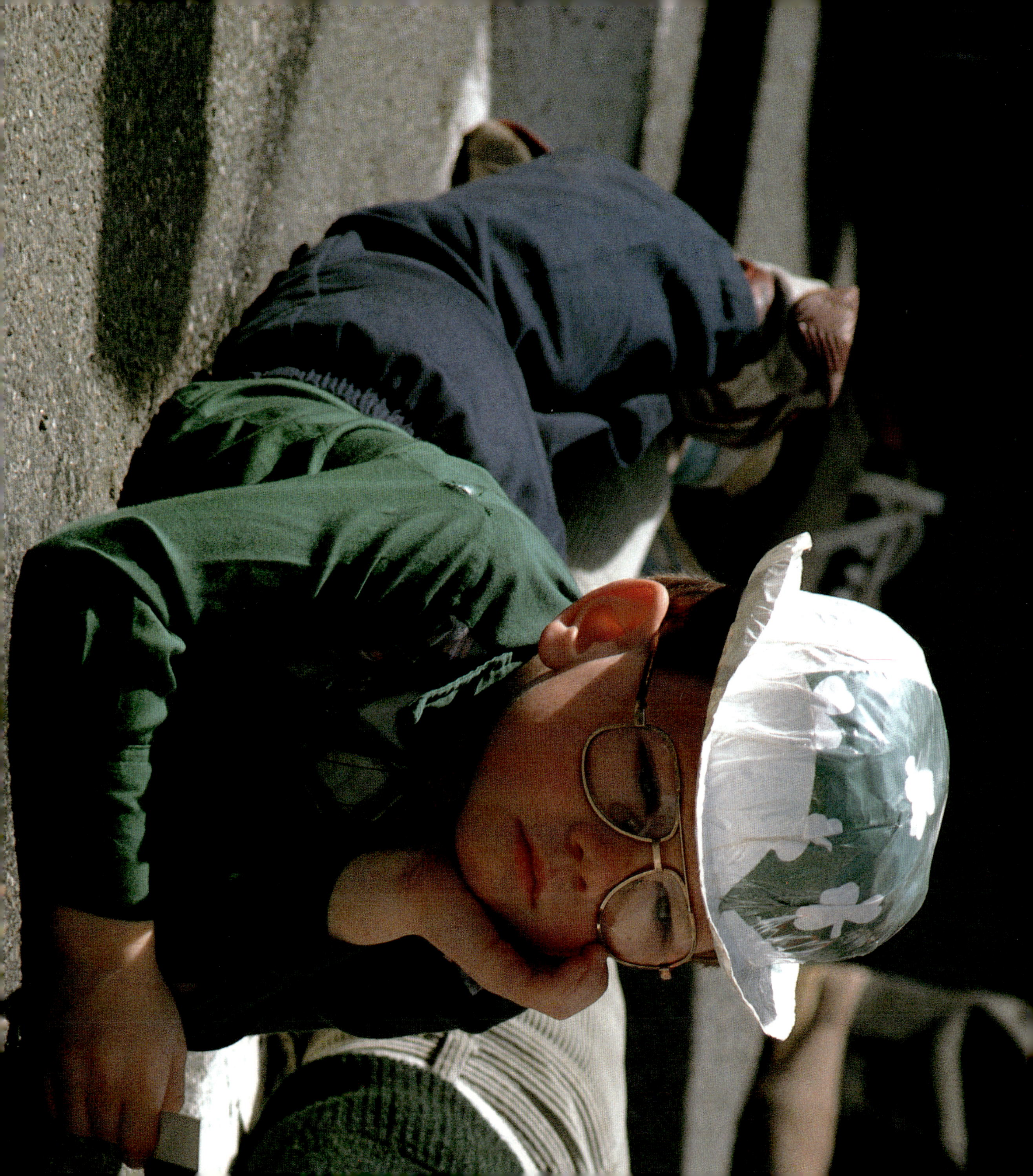

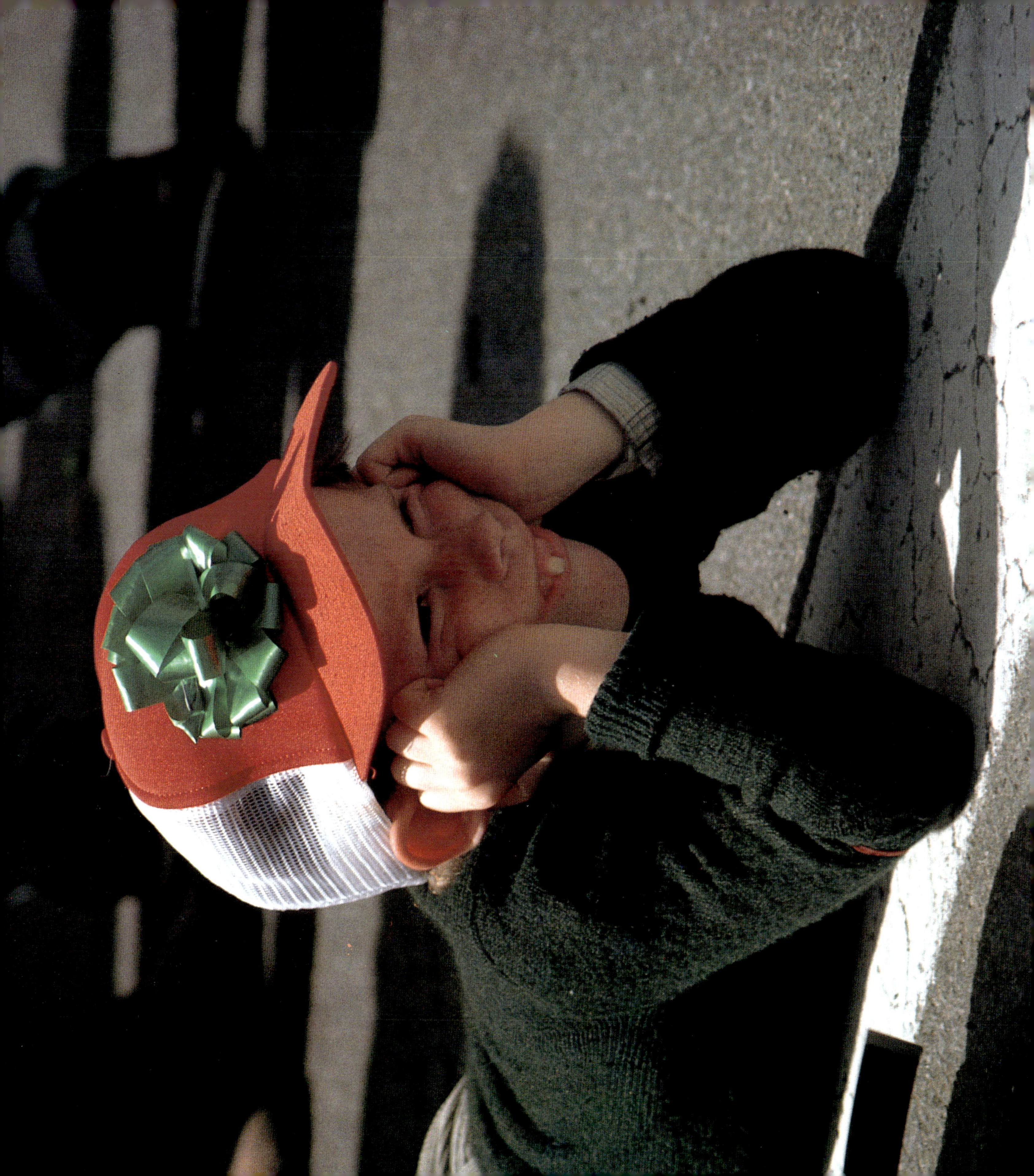

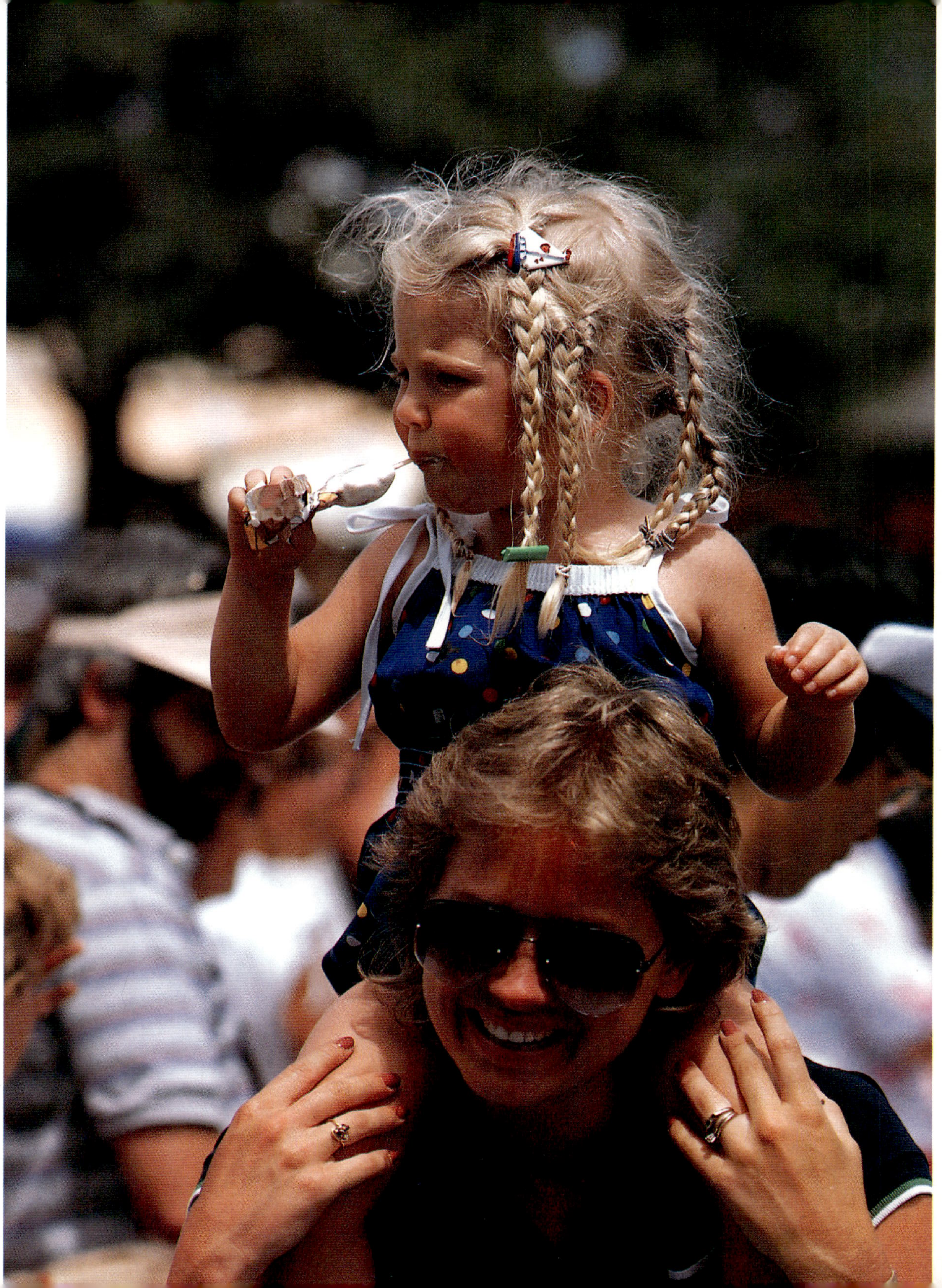

78 In San Francisco, everybody enjoys the pleasant climate and healthy out-of-doors lifestyle, and many families spend their leisure time in the Golden Gate Park away from the crowded streets and city traffic.

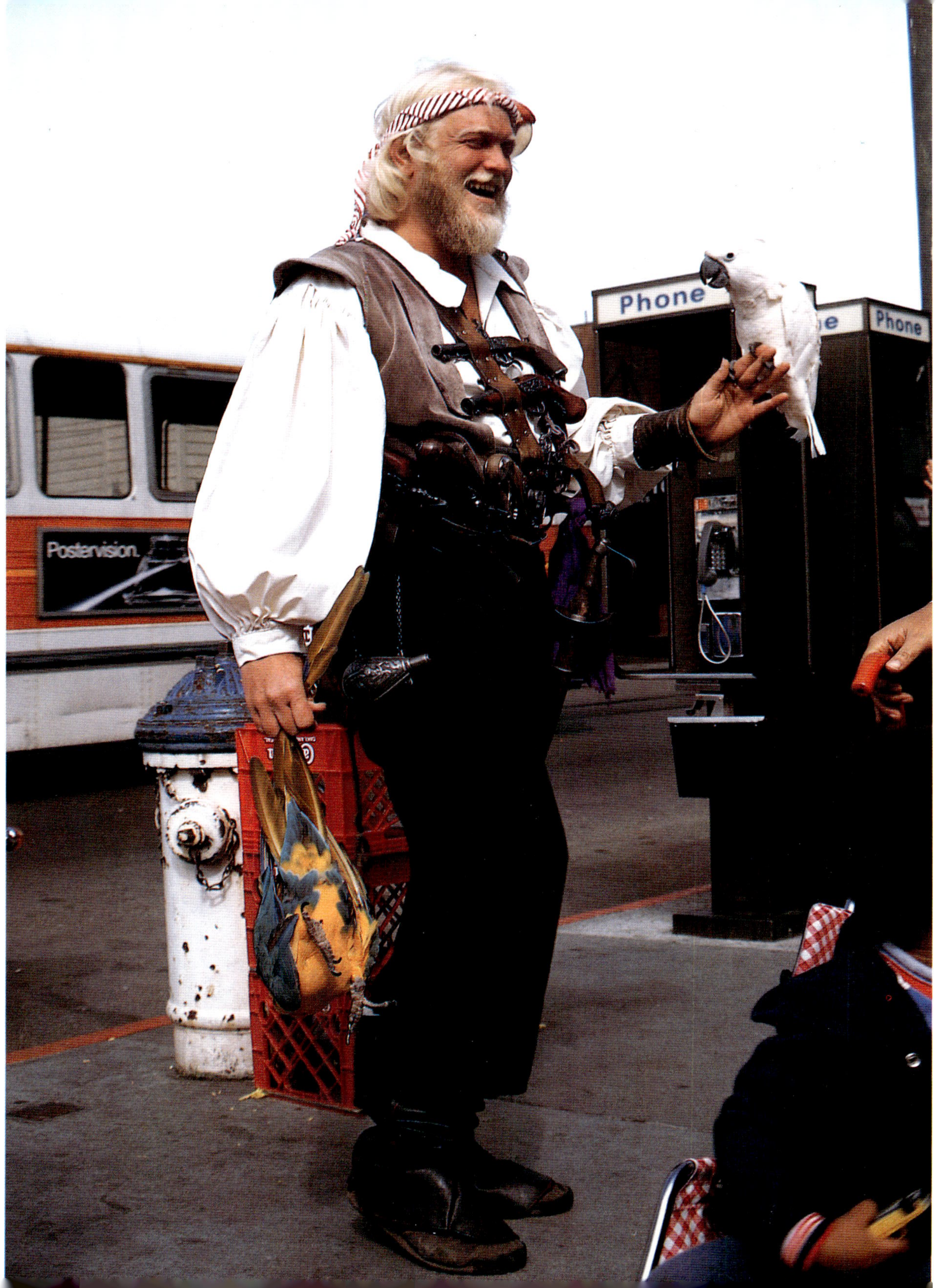

79 The city's streets, squares and parks abound with eccentric and original characters. It is not unusual to come across many impromptu and entertaining street shows, mime artists, jugglers and buskers.

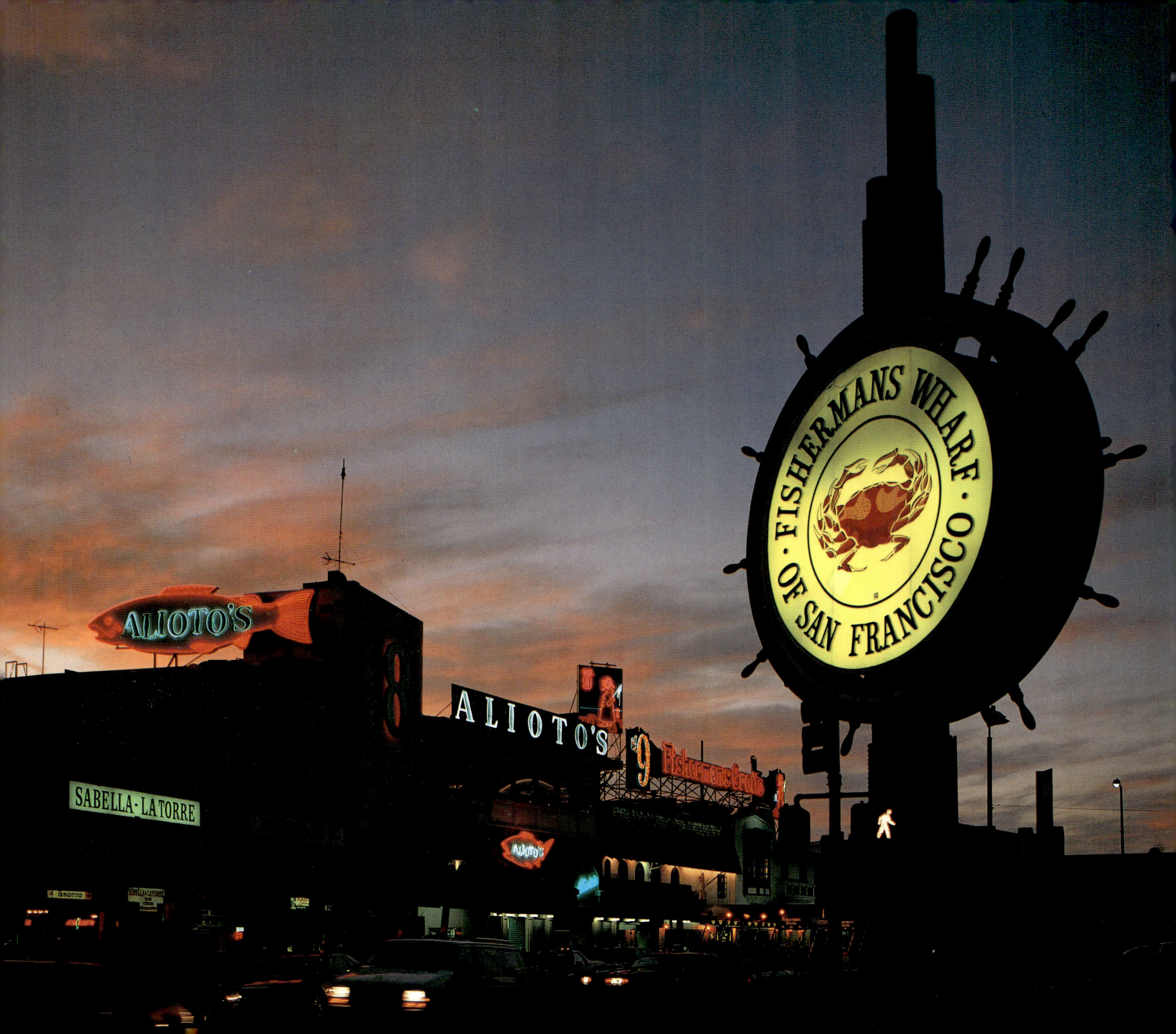
FISHERMANS WHARF · OF SAN FRANCISCO ·
ALIOTO'S
ALIOTO'S
SABELLA-LATORRE
9
Fishermans Grotto
8
GROTTO

80 Fisherman's Wharf was once San Francisco's fishing port but the area has been transformed over the last three decades and it is now renowned for its restaurants which specialize in seafood, particularly crabs and shrimps which are cooked in a variety of delicious ways.

81 Pier 39 is a popular venue for shopping and sightseeing and has many giftshops, craft galleries and restaurants clustered together in a wooden complex built in late nineteenth-century San Franciscan style. Constructed in 1978, the timber used was salvaged from demolished wharves within the port area.

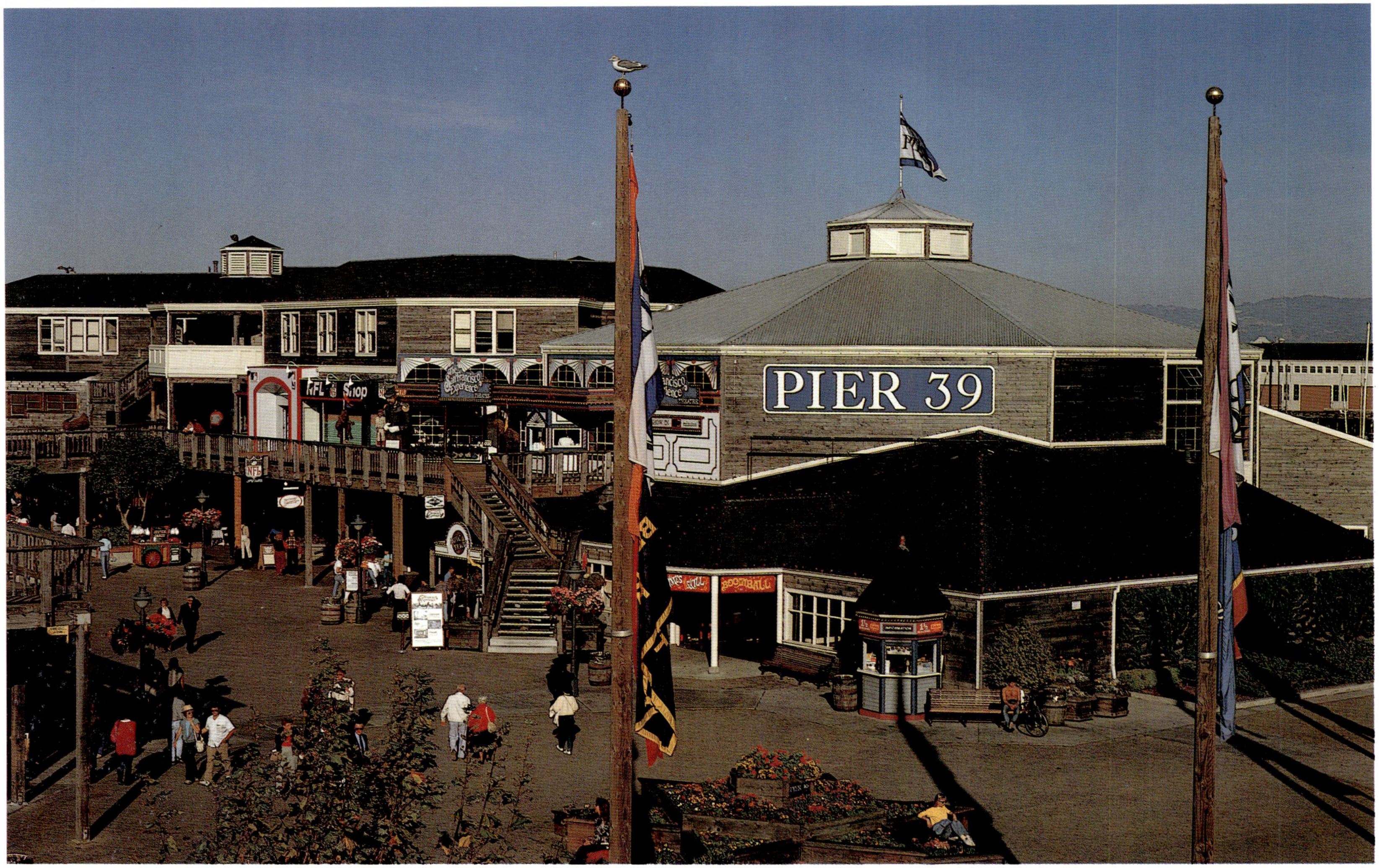

82-83 San Franciscans enjoy their city's nightlife. In addition to some fine restaurants, hotels and cabaret bars, there are some renowned theaters, concert halls and the world-famous San Francisco Opera. Theater and concert goers are spoilt for choice and support the arts enthusiastically.

84-85 At any time of day, the Golden Gate Bridge is a beautiful sight and a testament to Joseph Strauss's engineering skills and vision. It has become a powerful and enduring symbol of the City on the Bay.

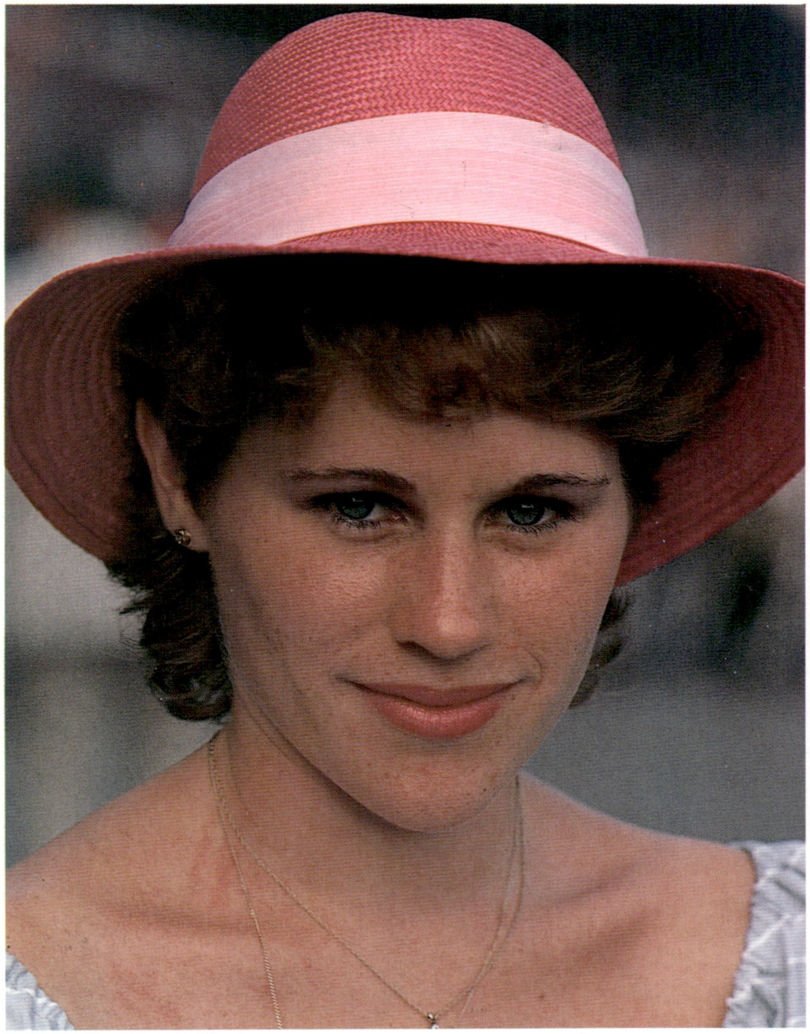

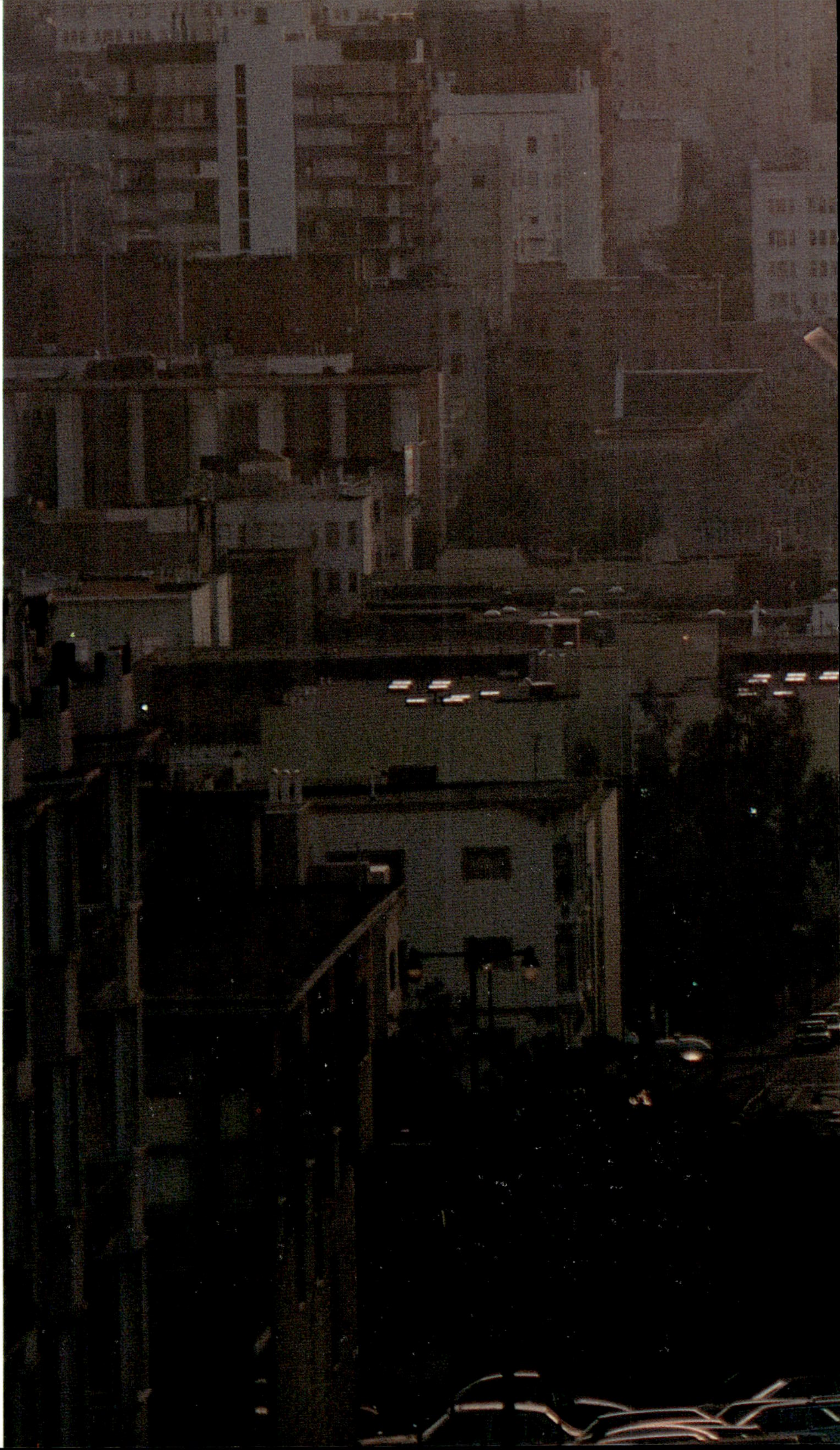

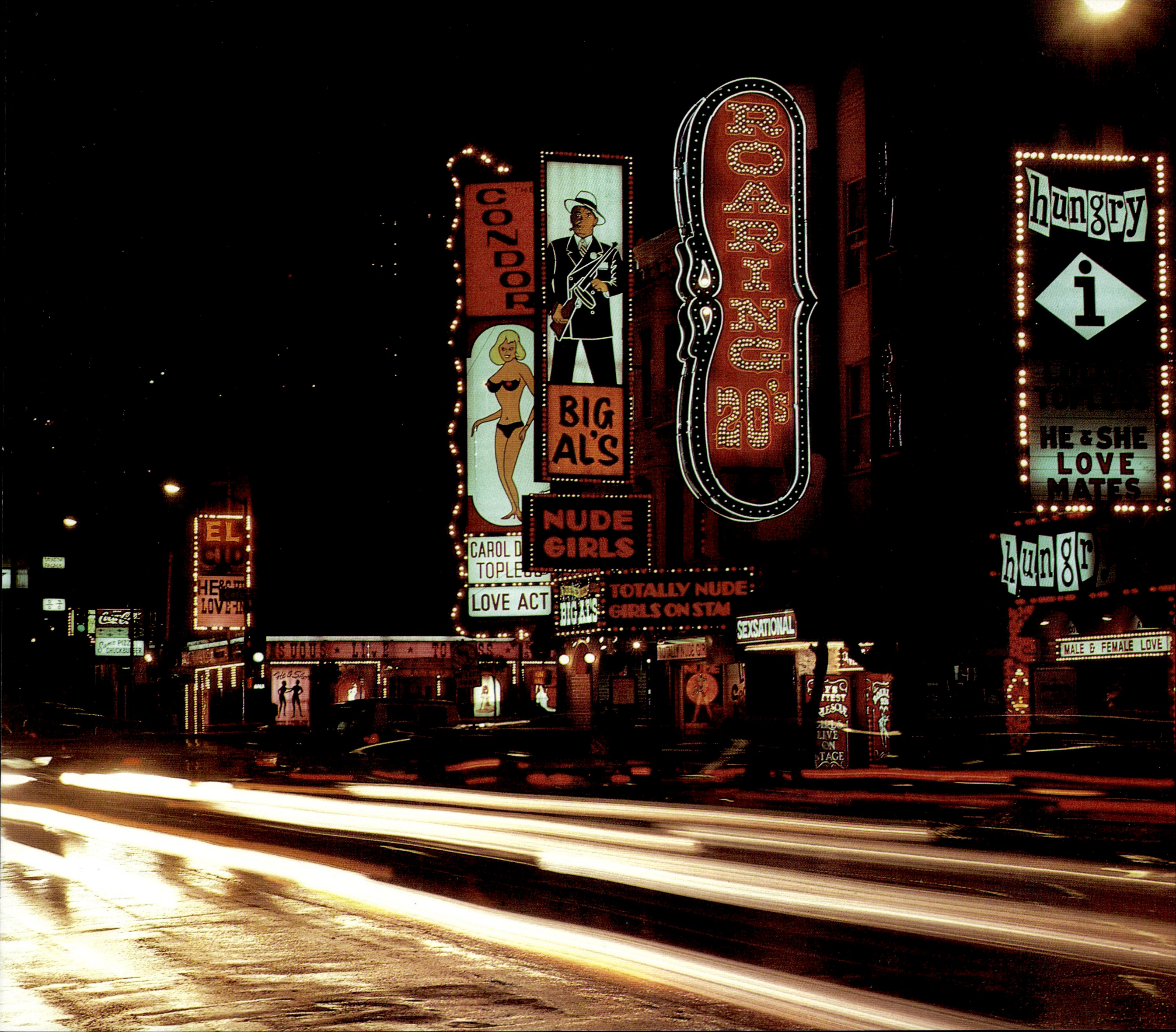

CONDOR
BIG AL'S
ROARING 20's
hungry
HE & SHE LOVE MATES
hungr
EL
NUDE GIRLS
LOVE ACT
TOTALLY NUDE
SEXSATIONAL
MALE & FEMALE LOVE
LIVE ON STAGE

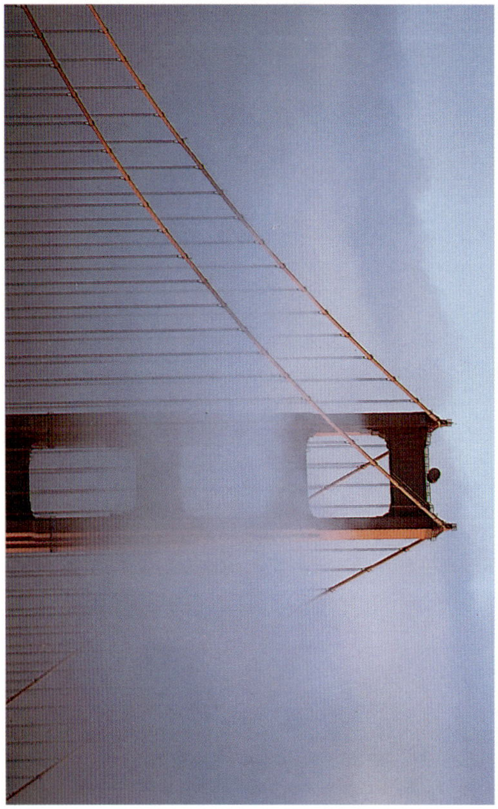